The 2011 season was special indeed... not only for our team, but for *everyone* with ties to the state of Alabama and the Crimson Tide Football Program. There are so many components to winning a National Championship; I would be remiss in not acknowledging all of the moving parts who played a considerable role in helping our players accomplish the *ultimate* goal in college football. From the President and Athletic Director; to the assistant coaches and support staff; to the best alumni and fans in the world; and, especially, to the loving and supportive families of us all... this one's for you!

High hopes abounded after the 2009 National Championship, however, a repeat in 2010 was not to be. Looking back, I believe the bowl game against Michigan State was clearly a turning point for the Crimson Tide. After a disappointing regular season, this team dug deep and found the fortitude to rebound and pledge their commitment to become the best they could be ... individually and collectively. Their dedication during Capital One Bowl practices paid dividends and, coupled with a sound 2011 4th Quarter Conditioning Program and Spring and Summer practices, the tone was set for Fall Camp and the season ahead. Then came the curve balls, which truly tested the character and spirit of our players. The devastating tornado of April 27th affected so many in Tuscaloosa and beyond. I couldn't be more proud of the way our team responded to those in need who, throughout the good, bad, and everything-in-between years, generously and enthusiastically supported the Crimson Tide. It was an opportunity to give back and, between a grueling academics and athletics schedule, our team *made* time to rebuild our communities, maintained a presence, and lent their support in any way they could to those who had lost someone or something. In May, we lost Aaron Douglas, a promising, up-and-coming offensive lineman. Even though Aaron had only been with us for a short time, he was 'one of our own' and a large contingent of players made the trip to Tennessee to celebrate his life and console his family. My message throughout these trying times was *that you cannot be a team only in the best of times ... you have to be a team when things are difficult as well.* The team more than answered that call and, as a result, was recognized in December with the Disney Spirit Award on the ESPN Awards show in Orlando ... a tremendous and very prestigious national honor. Yes, we were hailed as one of the top football teams in the country, however, more importantly, this award only confirmed how special these young men were *off* the turf...

The leadership of the 2011 team really came to fruition after our first regular season loss to LSU, hyped for weeks and dubbed by the media as *'The Game of the Century'* ... no pressure there! Without a doubt, it was a crushing defeat and my post-game address reiterated what I try to instill on a daily basis: execution and following through on the little things make all the difference in the end. The Crimson Tide could have easily packed it in for the rest of the season knowing full well that several scenarios beyond our wildest imagination would have to play out in order to create a rematch for the national title. It didn't matter, they continued to play with a 'won't be denied' attitude and that mettle was evident in stellar performances for the remainder of the season; the rest, as they say, is history! Our goal for the National Championship was *control your own destiny.* If we did what we needed to do, the outcome of the game would be determined by us and us alone. LSU² in New Orleans demonstrated the true character of our team and showed a tremendous amount of resiliency. Over and beyond some pretty remarkable game stats, even more noteworthy is that 21 of our players who had already graduated competed in the BCS National Championship Game ... placing us 2nd in the country behind Boise State. In addition to winning the title, this team set a conference record with 38 players on the SEC Academic Honor Roll ... that's a third of our team with a 3.0 GPA or better. Most impressive however, is the fact that we had the 2nd highest graduation rate in the Final BCS Top 10 behind Stanford, and were 2nd to Vanderbilt with highest graduation rate in the SEC. A coach's dream ... it was truly a privilege to coach these young men!

The 2011 season was one that many people will remember for a lot of reasons in terms of the adversity and challenges. It's easy to do the right thing some of the time, but this team, over the course of the year, did things right almost all of the time. The Crimson Tide played with a special purpose in 2011 and made Alabama's 14th National Championship even more memorable to so many Alabama fans and communities. **Roll Tide!**

TORNADO to NATIONAL TITLE #14

NATIONAL CHAMPIONS
CRIMSON TIDE
2011

Whitman Publishing, LLC
PUBLISHING SINCE 1934
www.whitman.com

Tornado To National Title #14

www.whitman.com
© 2012 Whitman Publishing, LLC

ISBN: 0794837387
Printed and assembled in the United States of America

TABLE OF
CONTENTS

IN MEMORY OF THOSE WE LOST

By TERRY SABAN

Football coaches live a gypsy life. When you lose, you move, and when you win, you move. Either way, you leave a trail of unsold houses and disgruntled children who can't order their class ring or try out for a spot on the cheerleading squad. Coaches' wives learn independence early on, exemplifying the quote found on needlepoint pillows, *"We Interrupt This Marriage For Football Season"* — all 12 months of it! However, football has been good to our family.

Nick and I married at 19, and it was our philosophy from the start that we would not continue in a profession that time and again leaves one packing up the Christmas tree into a box addressed to a different state, and a different team — unless it was a positive career move. Rather than move backward, we would use that business degree and buy a car dealership or gas station like Nick's father. And so it was, after 36 years and 16 moves, we find ourselves in the ultimate college town: Tuscaloosa, Alabama, home of the Crimson Tide and a proud 102,000-seat stadium saluted by bronze statues.

Perhaps it was the culture that so closely paralleled our upbringing in the coal-mining communities of West Virginia, or the rich football traditions that supersede entertainment and help shape the lives of young fans growing up. Perhaps it was the yearning for a return to excellence, a readiness for a tried-and-

true "process" that made us feel at home and confident that it would be a good fit for our family.

But none of the years of coaching prepared us for what happened in Tuscaloosa on April 27, 2011, not even the coal-mining disasters near our home in West Virginia where Nick's grandfather narrowly missed being one of the 86 miners forever entombed after the explosion at Monongah Mine. An EF-4 tornado, which deserved a name as infamous as any killer hurricane, mowed down a mile-wide path across the state of Alabama, claiming 253 lives and leaving what many called a "war zone" along the edge of campus. It showed no mercy as it flattened small communities, student housing and businesses. And after a month of search and rescue, funerals and tears, chain saws and bulldozers, six families took the long walk across the stage at graduation to accept the diplomas that their son or daughter should have held.

Immediately after the tornado, the stadium became a home for over a hundred rescue workers, the equipment managers washed hundreds of Red Cross blankets instead of football uniforms, and the team rallied around each other and the community to do whatever they could to heal the painful wounds. Whether it was taking water to workers or pounding nails, they gave of themselves. Our own Nick's Kids Fund charity, through many generous donations, was able to underwrite the rebuilding

4

of 14 homes. The outpouring of support crossed all Southeastern Conference lines as firefighters from Baton Rouge, Louisiana — who had left their jobs and homes to aid in the rescue — denied heroism and expressed to us, "You were there for us after Katrina."

Knowing such leadership and overcoming it strengthens the heart. Finding the courage to forget your own pain and reach out to others cleanses the soul and puts perspective on every aspect of our lives. It was the perspective that determined the following football season to be something special. Not only motivated by the usual pride of competition, this Tide team felt a yearning to do one more thing for the state of Alabama, a gift that might help them find some solace from the tragedies of their losses, a diversion from their pain — a national championship in which this state could take ownership.

History will look especially favorable on Alabama's 14th national championship as one that honored the memory of those lost in the tornado on April 27, 2011, and a football team that was determined to win for them. When members of this team bring their grandchildren back to the town they called home for four years — where many of them arrived as eager boys and left as graceful men — they might leave a red rose for a friend or loved one and remember them fondly as they whisper "Roll Tide."

— *Terry Saban, wife of Alabama head coach Nick Saban*

APRIL 27

A DAY

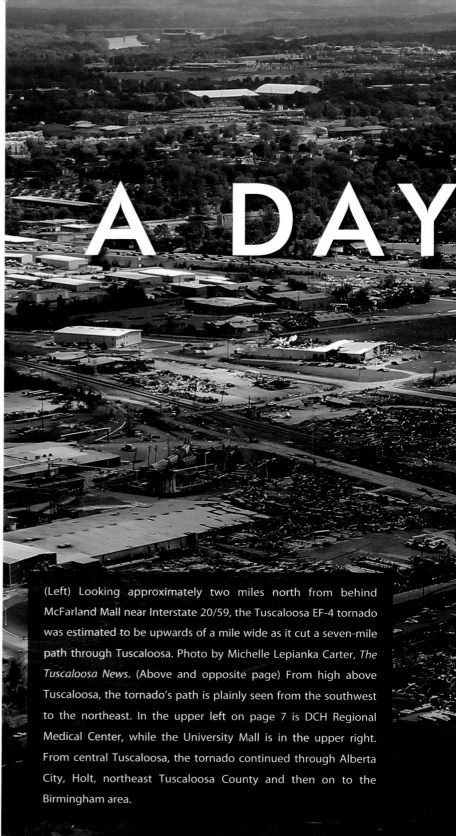

On Wednesday, April 27, 2011, residents of Tuscaloosa, Ala., awoke to an overcast, relatively quiet morning, even though thunderstorms were moving across other parts of the state and meteorologists had issued dire warnings of severe weather ahead.

No one could be blamed for responding to the predictions with at least some skepticism. After all, this was Tuscaloosa in the spring. Lightning-charged thunderstorms and tornadoes were nothing new. Less than two weeks earlier, for instance, a twister touched down south of town in an area where many University of Alabama faculty and staff have homes.

(Left) Looking approximately two miles north from behind McFarland Mall near Interstate 20/59, the Tuscaloosa EF-4 tornado was estimated to be upwards of a mile wide as it cut a seven-mile path through Tuscaloosa. Photo by Michelle Lepianka Carter, *The Tuscaloosa News*. (Above and opposite page) From high above Tuscaloosa, the tornado's path is plainly seen from the southwest to the northeast. In the upper left on page 7 is DCH Regional Medical Center, while the University Mall is in the upper right. From central Tuscaloosa, the tornado continued through Alberta City, Holt, northeast Tuscaloosa County and then on to the Birmingham area.

TO REMEMBER

One of the hardest hit neighborhoods in Tuscaloosa was Forest Lake, located just off 15th Street. In a matter of seconds, hundreds of residents were displaced.

That storm and others before it were dangerous enough, but not a surprise to local residents well acquainted with severe weather that is born in the Gulf of Mexico and routinely aimed at the Southeastern United States.

There was nothing ordinary, however, about the tornado that appeared just before 5 p.m. April 27 on a live feed from a video camera mounted atop the Tuscaloosa County Courthouse. Its sheer size seemed to shock even veteran weather forecasters who had done an excellent job of predicting the violent weather.

James Spann, a Birmingham television meteorologist known for his years of storm coverage, forcefully warned his ABC 33/40-TV audience watching in Tuscaloosa to brace for the worst, as did meteorologists also reporting live on other stations.

"This is a large, violent tornado coming up on downtown Tuscaloosa," Spann said. "Be in a safe place right now… That (tornado) is something you pray that you never, ever, ever see… This thing looks like it might be over one-half mile wide, maybe up to three-quarters of a mile wide… Get into a safe place!"

Spann's colleague, meteorologist Jason Simpson, told viewers, "That is something significantly wicked on the horizon of Tuscaloosa that is about to move into the city. It's large. It's violent."

The EF-4 wedge tornado cut a mile-wide path through the city, seven miles long from the southwest to the northeast, before continuing on another 80 miles through Birmingham's northern suburbs.

In Tuscaloosa alone, the massive twister killed 53 people — including six University of Alabama students — injured 1,200 others, and damaged or destroyed more than 5,300 homes and 350 businesses. And it was just one of a record 62 tornadoes that churned through Alabama on April 27, killing 253 people statewide.

For thousands of Alabamians, nothing would ever be the same. So, too, would it affect the University of Alabama's football team in a way that no one could have imagined. Although the team had finished spring practice and was gearing up for a run at its second Bowl Championship Series national title at that time, it suddenly had a far more important mission: To immediately pitch in and help storm victims in any way possible.

In doing so, they first had to reach out to one of their own.

As the tornado approached, Carson Tinker, a 6-foot-1, 220-pound junior long snapper for the Crimson Tide, rushed into a closet at his off-campus house with his girlfriend Ashley Harrison and held her tightly as the 190-mph winds hit. The next thing Tinker could remember, he was lying in a field 75 yards away. Harrison, a University of Alabama senior, was nowhere in sight among the twisted rubble where houses had stood seconds earlier.

Suffering from a broken wrist, concussion and a severe ankle injury, Tinker was taken to DCH Regional Medical Center, where he was later given the news that his girlfriend had been killed. The couple's two dogs also died in the storm.

Tinker's ordeal and his football team's response in helping Tuscaloosa recover from the storm would later earn them the

Within the Tuscaloosa city limits, more than 5,300 residences were damaged or destroyed, several of which were in Forest Lake. What the tornado itself didn't significantly damage, the trees did.

Disney Spirit Award, presented during the 2011 Home Depot College Football Awards show in Orlando. The tornado would also become a driving force behind the Crimson Tide's march to its second BCS title in three years and the program's 14th national championship overall.

"A lot of people hear my story and look at me and look at everything and expect me to have the 'poor mes'… but I don't," Tinker said during the ESPN-televised awards show in Orlando. "I have a positive attitude. And every day is a blessing. It's a gift from God, and I really try to take advantage of every day that I have."

Tinker "had to go through enormous healing of his own and contributed to a successful season and a BCS national championship victory," said Darlene Harrison, mother of Ashley Harrison, as the one-year anniversary of the storm approached. "Still,

By 10 a.m., he was speaking to a group of approximately 300 volunteers at the student center, saying, "Being part of a team is not always just being there on Saturday. Being a part of the University of Alabama team is to help people when they need it and there are a lot of people out there who need it.

"I want you to know I appreciate what you're doing."

From there, Saban went to the devastated 15th Street area and gave out water, Gatorade and ice, then traveled across town to the Belk Activity Center at Bowers Park where he met with hundreds of displaced storm victims.

After a trip to the UA student recreation center to visit with volunteers, he went to St. Mathias Church — the official City of Tuscaloosa volunteer location — then later that evening

(Left) The damage was extensive in Cedar Crest, with DCH Regional Medical Center in the background, and (below) Forest Lake.

he has never stopped finding ways to cherish the memory of Ashley."

As Tinker recovered in a Tuscaloosa hospital, his teammates and coaches reached out to hard-hit Tuscaloosa-area communities like Alberta, Rosedale and Holt.

Offensive lineman D.J. Fluker lost his off-campus home in Alberta to the storm, but like his teammates, devoted his time to helping others.

"I feel like, 'Hey, if I lost something, I've got to go help somebody else,'" Fluker said.

On Thursday, April 28, slightly over 12 hours after the storm, Alabama coach Nick Saban was in his office early, looking for ways to help. With no power in the building and spotty cell phone coverage, he and two staffers ventured out into the forever-changed landscape of Tuscaloosa.

(Below) With an eerie grayish-orange sky above, 15th Street near the Forest Lake area became a parking lot after the tornado came through. (Opposite page inset) At a workday near Soma Church in Holt, former Alabama football lettermen pause during the funeral procession of Jennifer Bayode, who was killed by the tornado in her Holt home.

returned to the Belk Center and, along with wife Terry, helped feed some 700 tornado victims.

It was the beginning of a massive effort from Saban and his team as they responded with as much dedication to the city's recovery over the next year as they would any battle on the football field.

President Barack Obama, visiting Tuscaloosa on Friday, April 29, summed up the raw feelings of those who saw the damage firsthand.

"I've got to say, I've never seen devastation like this," Obama said. "It is heartbreaking. What you're seeing here is the consequence of just a few minutes of this extraordinarily powerful storm sweeping through this community. As the governor (Robert Bentley) was mentioning, Tuscaloosa usually gets a tornado during the season but this is something I don't think anybody's seen before."

Only later would it be revealed that the president had given the order that morning, just before he boarded Air Force One to fly to Tuscaloosa, to go forward with a mission to capture or kill terrorist Osama bin Laden in a Pakistani hideout halfway around the world. Two days later, bin Laden was dead.

While the nation breathed a sigh of relief over the success of the mission, Alabama residents were struggling with an unprecedented natural disaster.

"It's the most devastating thing I've seen in my life," Saban said a week after the storm during an address to Crimson Caravan attendees in suburban Birmingham. "But we will build a better place."

And for the next year, he and his team set about doing just that. Nick's Kids, the charitable foundation established by Saban and his wife Terry, immediately turned its focus to tornado relief, directing more than $1 million to rebuilding efforts in partnership with Habitat for Humanity (for building projects), Project Team Up (for cleanup efforts) and Tuscaloosa Tornado Relief.

The group also helped rebuild a playground in Phil Campbell, a small town practically destroyed by one of the tornadoes that swept across the state.

In an inspiring tie-in to football history, Nick's Kids partnered with Habitat for Humanity to rebuild 13 houses to match the Crimson Tide's national championship total. The "13 for 13" project had to be amended following Alabama's 21-0 BCS National Championship Game victory over LSU in New Orleans on Jan. 9, 2012. A 14th house was added to the plan.

Alabama's team, however, was far from alone among college football programs that pitched in to help those suffering from the single largest natural disaster to ever strike the state. A contingent of 70 Auburn football players, coaches and staff boarded buses the morning of Friday, April 29, to help tornado victims in the Alabama towns of Cullman and Pleasant Grove, two of the hardest hit areas in the state.

(Preceding page, top) Pam Rogers, a volunteer for the American Red Cross, welcomes Alabama coach Nick Saban to the Belk Center at Bowers Park. (Preceding page, bottom left) Pam Rogers and Coach Saban prepare to feed some 700 persons displaced by the tornado. (Preceding page, bottom right) Coach Saban and wife Terry greet an Alabama fan. (Below) Coach Saban provides comfort for a displaced tornado victim.

"It was devastating," Auburn head coach Gene Chizik said in a statement released after his team's visit. "I don't even think you can accurately describe the enormity, you have to see it. To see families displaced, lives lost, this is absolutely tragic."

The Auburn Football Lettermen Club immediately called on members to make donations "for our friends in Tuscaloosa."

And perhaps most importantly, given the intense football rivalry between Alabama and Auburn, a group of War Eagle fans calling themselves "Toomer's for Tuscaloosa" organized quickly to aid in the relief effort. Their number of volunteers skyrocketed within months, as the group helped to rebuild homes, operate relief centers and serve what amounted to more than 80,000 meals to tornado victims.

"Toomer's for Tuscaloosa" proved to be so successful as a grass-roots organization that it ultimately expanded to help storm victims in Joplin, Mo., and other areas.

Fans of other teams, including the LSU faithful who were members of the Louisiana Task Force Search and Rescue Team, also rushed to Tuscaloosa to help out.

And players from Kent State University, Coach Saban's alma mater and the Crimson Tide's first football opponent in 2011, took time out from their summer as well to rebuild houses.

"My heart was feeling for all the victims of the tornado," Kent State running back Jacquise Terry said as he and his teammates hammered nails on a hot July day in Tuscaloosa.

Alabama offensive lineman D.J. Fluker, working with the Kent State players that day, said, "I feel honored because they actually took time to come down here and help us out."

"It was the right thing to do," Kent State Assistant Athletic Director Alan Ashby said. "Coach Saban and his wife Terry both being Kent State graduates. It kind of made sense."

Saban praised his alma mater for its efforts.

"It makes me proud that I went to Kent State," he said. "We really appreciate what these young guys are doing, probably more than they know. It's a tribute to the character that they have at the school and in their program that they would have young men who would sacrifice two or three days to come down here and help the people of Tuscaloosa rebuild this community."

(Top left) Coach Saban, a Kent State alumnus, chats with three Kent State football players at a workday in Holt. (Top right) As a joint project between the Nick's Kids Fund and Habitat for Humanity, Coach Saban kicks off the "13 for 13" home-building project (it was later changed to "14 for 14").

For their efforts, Kent State football players received a standing ovation from Alabama fans upon entering Bryant-Denny Stadium for the opening game of the season on Sept. 3, 2011.

In a letter to *The Birmingham News* following his team's 48-7 loss to the Crimson Tide that day, Kent State Athletic Director Joel Nielsen commended Alabama players and their fans.

The ovation "was something unheard of at a college football game, and speaks volumes about the citizens of Alabama and Crimson Tide fans everywhere," Nielsen wrote. "From the bottom of our hearts, thank you for opening your arms to our players in July and again to our team and fans this past weekend. It was an experience none of us will soon forget, and even more important in this time of extreme negativity, it was a perfect illustration of all that can be right with college athletics."

Other help came in the form of financial contributions, including a $500,000 donation from the Southeastern Conference for relief efforts. The Crimson Tide's own Athletic Department donated $1 million to the University of Alabama's Acts of Kindness Fund, created to help UA students, faculty and staff who were directly impacted by the tornado.

Other contributions came pouring in from celebrities, including singer Taylor Swift's $250,000 donation to Nick's Kids for the foundation's tornado relief efforts. A $400,000 donation from the Alabama-based Drummond Company was also distributed through Nick's Kids for the Habitat for Humanity building projects.

At an Aug. 28, 2011, memorial service on campus, Saban offered condolences to the families of the six Alabama students lost in the tragedy, along with the loved ones of those killed statewide. He also expressed hope that the coming football season might offer hope to those who had spent so many weeks struggling to recover.

(Above) Led by strength and conditioning coach Scott Cochran, more than 40 Alabama football players volunteered for cleanup duties in Holt. In total in Tuscaloosa and Tuscaloosa County, an estimated 1.5 million cubic yards of debris was removed, enough to fill Bryant-Denny Stadium five times.

"The spirit that we have at this university, that passion that we have for football, is something that can be a little bit of a diversion from what we all have to do to rebuild our community," Saban said. "I also think it can continue to create a tremendous awareness on a national level of everyone who comes to see one of our games, of what they might be able to do to help our community and to do something additional to help our community rebuild itself.

"We will wear a ribbon on our helmets in every game to honor all those we memorialize, as well as all those who have been affected and devastated by this storm, as well as all those who have supported the community."

Although the Crimson Tide would shoulder the hopes and dreams of a university, a city and a state as it played inspired football in 2011, it was clear that the team's most important victory was already sealed before the season began.

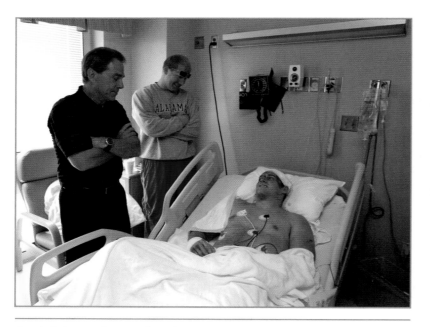

Coach Saban and strength and conditioning coach Scott Cochran visit long snapper Carson Tinker at DCH Regional Medical Center.

Coach Saban speaks to volunteers at St. Mathias Church.

Former Alabama head coach Gene Stallings greets Saban at St. Mathias Church.

Saban gives instructions to Alabama players Milton Talbert, Brandon Gibson, John Fulton, Harrison Jones and Barrett Jones.

THE MARCH TO THE
NATIONAL TITLE

48
Alabama
Kent State
7

YEAR IN AND YEAR OUT. WE JUST WANTED TO GO OUT AND EXECUTE." - COURTNEY UPSHAW

"IT'S ALWAYS GOOD TO GET A WIN UNDER YOUR BELT"

K
SEPT3
VS. KENT STATE

GAME 01 RECAP

NO. 2 ALABAMA FOOTBALL TEAM OPENED THE 2011 SEASON WITH A 48-7 WIN OVER THE KENT STATE GOLDEN FLASHES BEFORE A SOLD-OUT CROWD OF 101,821 AT BRYANT-DENNY STADIUM.

#2

A

K

48

PLEASANT

WE RAN A LOT OF GOOD PLAYS, AND WE HAD A LOT OF PLAYERS GET EXPERIENCE. THAT EXPERIENCE A LOT OF OPPORTUNITIES

WE ALL CAME OUT AND WANTED TO DOMINATE. ...WE ARE HELD TO A HIGH STANDARD HERE, BEING FROM ALABAMA. THE WAY OUR DEFENSE IS FROM

OFFENSE	SPECIAL TEAMS	DEFENSE
75 JONES	33 DEPRIEST*	24 MENZIE
42 LACY	29 LOWERY	41 UPSHAW
	4 MAZE**	
	3 SUNSERI	

*SEC FRESHMAN OF THE WEEK

**SEC HONORABLE MENTION

WE LIVE IT.

FOR OUR YOUNG GUYS THAT PLAY CRITICAL POSITIONS." - NICK SABAN

After 129 grueling days that saw death, destruction and dreams shattered — yet an unprecedented spirit of pride, love and service — Sept. 3, 2011, could not get to Tuscaloosa soon enough.

It was finally — to borrow a gem from baseball vernacular — time to play ball.

"We're very excited to open the season for a lot of different reasons," Alabama head coach Nick Saban said a few days before the Crimson Tide's home-opening win, "(one of which is) for the sake of our community from the standpoint of giving people — from a spiritual standpoint — something else to think about, something else to be passionate about, something else to create hope about and to continue to create awareness for the community. A lot of people are going to come to the game and see Tuscaloosa for the first time. Maybe that will inspire some people to continue to try to help rebuild our community."

The Tide's 48-7 blowout of Kent State was far from the typical home opener. As Saban alluded, for many people, the trip to Tuscaloosa was their first since the April 27 tornado, and no one knew quite what to expect. Despite what they had heard, or the images they had seen, nothing could have prepared them for what awaited.

Routes to Bryant-Denny Stadium were the same, but many familiar landmarks were gone. The busiest intersection in Tuscaloosa — 15th Street and McFarland Boulevard (considered the tornado's "Ground Zero") — bore no resemblance to its pre-tornado days. Hargrove Road and 15th Street into the outskirts of campus were shells of themselves. The areas around Tenth Avenue in the Rosedale area — a major route into the south end of Bryant-Denny — were filled with rubble, twisted steel and trees with stripped-away foliage.

(Preceding page) After every 2011 Crimson Tide victory, University of Alabama Athletics Department director of photography Kent Gidley designed a poster that hung throughout the football building the week following the game. (Below) Not only were giant houndstooth ribbons on the field for the season opener, but also on flags to honor the tornado victims.

Alabama Gov. Robert Bentley thanks Edgar Calloway during pregame ceremonies that honored the tornado's first responders who put their lives on the line to save others.

A GAME THAT MATTERED:

LSU, ranked fourth in the Associated Press poll, defeated third-ranked Oregon 40-27 in Dallas, Texas.

It was indeed a day of *"This is Alabama Football,"* but with a definitive asterisk.

In heartfelt pregame ceremonies, the university, along with Alabama Gov. Robert Bentley, honored the tornado's first responders who put their lives on the line to save others. Mal Moore, Alabama's athletic director, said they "represent the best of what we are all about as a state and a community."

As the players trotted onto the pristine field adorned by giant houndstooth ribbons, roaring cheers went up for both squads. Special recognition went to the visiting Kent State players, several of whom spent an extended July weekend in Tuscaloosa assisting with tornado-relief efforts. For Saban, a defensive back for Kent State from 1970-72, this game took on special meaning.

From start to finish, the second-ranked Tide dominated the Golden Flashes. With quarterbacks A.J. McCarron and Phillip Sims splitting time, Bama's offense piled up 482 yards while limiting Kent State to just 90 yards, including negative 9 yards rushing. Defensively, it was the Tide's second-best performance under Saban.

McCarron, whose performance earned him the starting quarterback job, completed 14 of 23 passes for 226 yards and two touchdowns while senior Marquis Maze led all receivers with 118 yards on eight receptions and a touchdown. Maze also added 135 return yards on special teams for 253 all-purpose yards. Running backs Jalston Fowler, Eddie Lacy and Trent Richardson led the Tide's 183-yard rushing effort.

"Obviously, it was a good win for us," Saban said following the game. "It's always good to get a win under your belt. There were a lot of things that we did well today. We ran a lot of good plays, and we had a lot of players get experience. That experience also brings a lot of learning opportunities for our young guys that play critical positions. We have a lot to learn and a lot of things we can improve on."

Alabama defensive coordinator Kirby Smart and head coach Nick Saban on the headphones during the Kent State game.

(Top) Carson Tinker, left, and Brad Smelley charge down the field against the Golden Flashes. (Above) Quarterback A.J. McCarron prepares to pass while offensive tackle Barrett Jones blocks his man.

(Above) Wide receiver Marquis Maze reaches out to make a fingertip catch. (Right inset) Cornerback Dre Kirkpatrick displays tight coverage against Kent State.

(Left) Running back Eddie Lacy battles for some of his 134 total yards. (Below) Linebacker Dont'a Hightower wraps up Kent State quarterback Spencer Keith.

Linebacker C.J. Mosley sacks the KSU quarterback.

GAME 2

HARD NOSED

SEPT 10
VS. PENN STATE

OLD-FASHIONED

PHYSICAL

FOOTBALL

GAME

GAME
2 SEPT. 10
2011

GAME 02 RECAP

STATE COLLEGE, PA. · THE NO. 3 ... FOOTBALL TEAM (2-0) CAME AWAY WITH ... VICTORY OVER THE 23RD-RANKED ... STATE NITTANY LIONS (1-1) ON ... DAY AT BEAVER STADIUM BEFORE ... CROWD OF 107,846. THE CRIMSON TIDE HAD 359 YARDS OF TOTAL OFFENSE, 194 RUSHING AND 165 RECEIVING, WHILE THE DEFENSE FORCED A PAIR OF FUMBLES AND COLLECTED ONE INTERCEPTION IN ... GAME. THE TIDE DEFENSE LIMITED ... NITTANY LIONS TO 250 TOTAL YARDS ... RUSHING, 144 PASSING) MARKING ... 31ST TIME IN 56 GAMES UNDER ALABAMA HEAD COACH NICK SABAN THAT THE OPPOSITION HAS COLLECTED ... THAN 300 YARDS OF TOTAL ... ENSE.

#3

#23

27

11

27
Alabama
Penn State
11

"WHETHER DIFFERENT GUYS ARE GOING IN THERE OR NOT, IT'S ALL ABOUT EVERYONE JUST DOING THEIR JOB."
- WILLIAM VLACHOS

OFFENSE

SPECIAL TEAMS

DEFENSE

73 VLACHOS**	**33** DePRIEST	**4** BARRON*
89 WILLIAMS	**28** MILLINER	**21** KIRKPATRICK
	3 SUNSERI	**32** MOSLEY
	91 WATKINS	

**SEC HONORABLE MENTION

*SEC PLAYER OF THE WEEK

WE LIVE IT.

No one could know it at the time, but Penn State head coach Joe Paterno's 14th game against Alabama would turn out to be his last in the series and his final loss in college football.

The fact that Alabama won 27-11 in front of the largest crowd to ever see the Crimson Tide play seemed anti-climactic considering the almost surreal events that preceded and followed this game.

The drama began a week before kickoff when torrential rains from Tropical Storm Lee flooded rivers and highways all around State College, Pa., site of the game, making travel hazardous for fans. Areas that averaged 1 inch of rain in September received up to 15 inches. Nevertheless, they poured into Happy Valley as the weekend progressed, welcomed by sunny skies and mid-70-degree temperatures.

By game day, Penn State's "Whiteout in the Whitehouse" promotion was in full force. The marketing ploy, in which fans turn out in a sea of white, was nothing new to the Crimson Tide. Three years earlier in 2008, Alabama had spoiled Georgia's "Blackout" in Athens, Ga., rolling to a 31-0 first-half lead en route to a 41-30 victory. In Beaver Stadium, the sight of more than 100,000 fans in all-white was impressive, but it was the *team* in white that dominated the day.

The third-ranked Tide — having been replaced by LSU in the No. 2 poll spot — rolled to 359 yards of total offense (196 rushing and 163 receiving), while the defense forced a pair of fumbles, collected one interception and held Penn State to 251 total yards.

Penn State scored first on a 43-yard field goal, but from there Alabama posted 27 straight points, holding the Nittany Lions scoreless until the end of the fourth quarter. Penn State closed out the game with a touchdown and successful two-point conversion in the final two minutes, long after the outcome had been decided.

The Tide's Trent Richardson rushed for 111 yards and a pair of touchdowns, with Eddie Lacy adding another 85 yards on the ground. Quarterback A.J. McCarron completed 19 of 31 passes for 163 yards and one touchdown.

For the sophomore McCarron, it was somewhat of a coming-out party. After splitting snaps with Phillip Sims the previous week against Kent State, McCarron was efficient, precise and unrattled in his performance before a hostile crowd. While the Nittany Lions were struggling to solve their quarterback quandary, McCarron assumed not only the starter's role for the Tide, but a leadership and confidence role as well.

"A.J. did a really good job today in managing the game, taking what the defense gave him and making enough plays in the passing game," Alabama coach Nick Saban said. "He was good today. He did a nice job. He showed leadership and confidence. He distributed the ball."

(Below) Quarterback A.J. McCarron had a coming-out party at Penn State.

McCarron's tone-setting performance started late in the first quarter. Down 3-0, on the Tide's second drive McCarron completed five of six passes for 59 yards, including a 5-yard bullet strike — in between two Penn State defenders — to tight end Michael Williams. The touchdown was a clear momentum-changer for both squads.

"I think I managed the game a lot better today," said McCarron, who had thrown two interceptions the previous week against Kent State. "The whole offense did a great job of not allowing turnovers and the defense got us turnovers. If we keep playing like that, we're going to be a special team."

Safety Mark Barron and linebacker C.J. Mosley led the rock-solid Alabama defense with seven total tackles each, while cornerback Dre Kirkpatrick was responsible for both forced Penn State fumbles.

Alabama's victory dropped Paterno's all-time record against the Tide to 4-10. His four wins all came during the schools'

(Above) Wide receiver Kevin Norwood knocks the helmet off Penn State defensive back Nick Sukay.

10-year series from 1981-90 — 1983, 1985, 1986 and 1990. Alabama's 10 wins came in 1981, 1982 (Penn State's only loss in its national championship season), 1984, 1987, 1988, 1989, 2010, 2011 and in the Sugar Bowl following the 1975 and 1978 seasons.

Following the Alabama game, Paterno coached the Nittany Lions to seven more victories before being fired Nov. 8 after allegations of child abuse were reported — and later proven in a court of law — against his former defensive coordinator, Jerry Sandusky.

Shortly after his dismissal, Paterno's family announced he had been diagnosed with a treatable form of lung cancer. A little more than two months later, however, on Jan. 22, 2012, the 85-year-old Paterno died.

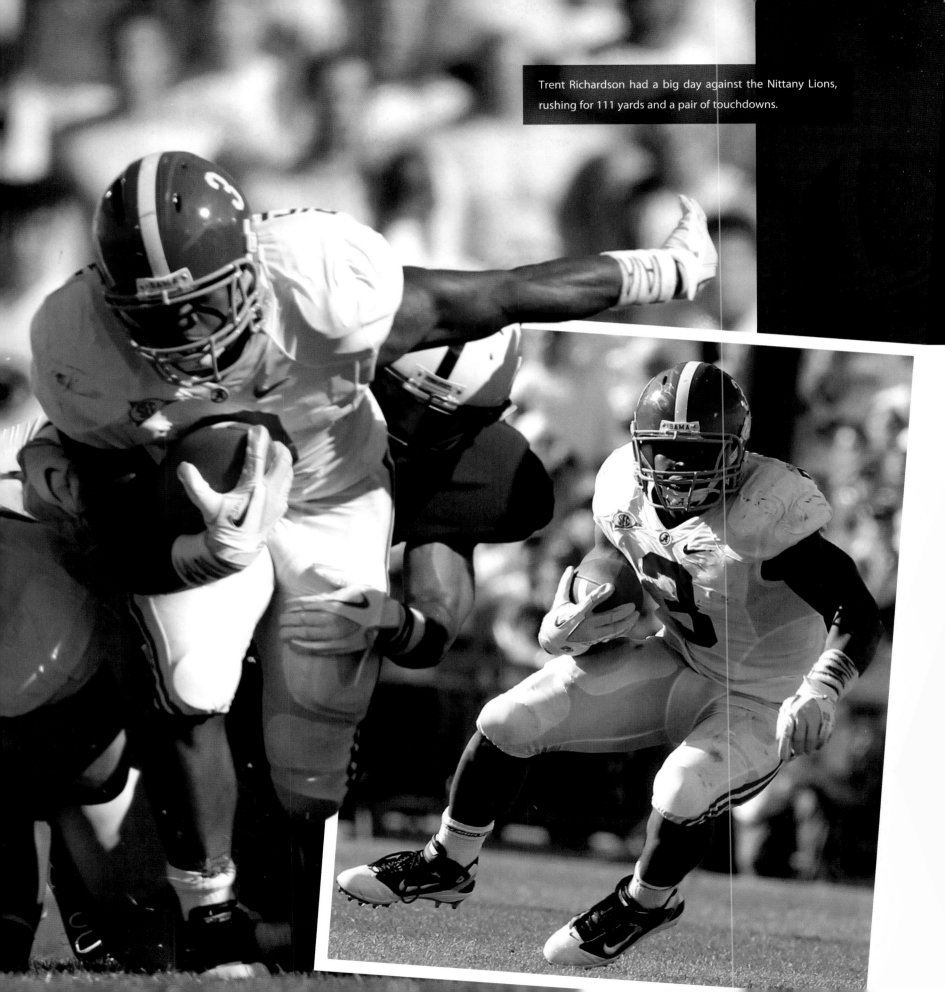

Trent Richardson had a big day against the Nittany Lions, rushing for 111 yards and a pair of touchdowns.

(Above) Defensive back Robert Lester attempts to deflect a pass by Penn State quarterback Matt McGloin. (Left inset) Marquis Maze tries to elude Penn State linebacker Michael Mauti.

Eddie Lacy drags three PSU defenders with him on the way to 85 rushing yards on the day.

Tight end Michael Williams catches a 5-yard touchdown pass in the first quarter.

Courtney Upshaw prepares to rush the quarterback.

(Top) Dont'a Hightower, left, and Jesse Williams can sense the victory is at hand. (Above) Head coach Nick Saban chats with ESPN after the 27-11 win.

BEST WE CAN BE. THAT IS OUR GOAL ON DEFENSE, HOW GOOD CAN WE BE." - DAMION SQUARE

BREAKING FREE
IN BRYANT-DENNY

GAME **03** RECAP

TUSCALOOSA, ALA. - THE ALABAMA FOOTBALL TEAM DOM NORTH TEXAS ON BOTH SIDES FOOTBALL SATURDAY NIGHT E TO A 41-0 VICTORY BEFORE 1 BRYANT-DENNY STADIUM. THE TIDE TOTALED 586 YARDS AS JUNIOR RUNNING BAC ARDSON AND SOPHOM BACK EDDIE LACY BOT CAREER-HIGH RUSHI ARDSON FINISHED TH 167 YARDS ON 11 CAR THREE TOUCHDOWNS, WHIL ADDED 161 YARDS ON NINE CARRIES AND TWO TOUCHDOWNS.

"IT ALWAYS FEELS GOOD TO RUN BEHIND THE OFFENSIVE LINE LIKE THAT. TO BREAK FREE IN BRYANT-DENNY IS ALWAYS A GOOD FEELING." -TRENT RICHARDSON

"FOR EVERYTHING TO GO RIGHT WE HAVE TO EXECUTE ON DEFENSE AND EXECUTE OUR ASSIGNMENTS NO MATTER WHO WE PLAY. IT'S ALL ABOUT BEING THE BEST WE

#2

OFFENSE	P	TEAMS	DEFENSE
42 LACY		RIS	4 BARRON
3 RICHARDSON**		WERY	30 HIGHTOWER
			37 LESTER
			41 UPSHAW**

**SEC HONORABLE MENTION

WE LIVE IT.

GAME
3 SEPT. 17
2011

41
Alabama
North Texas
0

Throughout the history of Bryant-Denny Stadium, all kinds of teams with all sorts of nicknames have rolled through, each trying to give the Crimson Tide their best shot.

In zoo-like fashion, there have been Lions, Tigers, Wildcats and Gators. Eagles, Gamecocks, Bearcats, Bulldogs and Razorbacks have all battled Alabama on the turf. There have even been uprisings by Rebels and Blue Devils, Commodores and Scarlet Knights, and Volunteers through the years. Cougars, Wolves, Warhawks and Blue Raiders have appeared in Tuscaloosa.

Then, there's the North Texas Mean Green, with perhaps the most unique nickname of all. The school's 1966 squad was dubbed the "Mean Green" because of its nationally ranked defense. On the line was Joe Greene, a future college and pro hall of fame member who would pick up the nickname "Mean Joe Greene" as a Pittsburgh Steelers rookie in 1969. By then, the "Mean Green" nickname had been permanently adopted by North Texas.

The Crimson Tide's third win on its march to the 2011 national championship — a 41-0 drubbing of North Texas — proved one thing: the Mean Green didn't quite live up to its nickname. The Tide, now back up to No. 2 in the polls, dominated on both sides of the ball, holding the Mean Green to just 91 yards of offense while totaling 586 yards of its own. Trent Richardson (167 yards on 11 carries) and Eddie Lacy (161 yards on nine carries) rushed for career highs, and in doing so, they became the first duo in Tide history to rush for more than 150 yards in the same game.

"It's obviously good to win," Alabama head coach Nick Saban said after the Tide ran its record to a perfect 4-0 against North Texas. "I think the goal of what we are trying to do is improve as a team."

After three games, a 3-0 record and a No. 2 national ranking behind No. 1 Oklahoma, it was time for the Tide to turn its attention to bigger and better goals, starting with Southeastern Conference rival Arkansas.

(Right) Trent Richardson steps into the end zone against North Texas.

Eddie Lacy grabs the jersey of teammate Brad Smelley while trying to maneuver between two North Texas defenders.

North Texas quarterback Derek Thompson prepares to pass while Dont'a Hightower, C.J. Mosley and Courtney Upshaw collapse the pocket.

(Top right) Defensive back Will Lowery makes sure his man isn't going anywhere. (Bottom right) Tight end Brad Smelley gets upended after a catch.

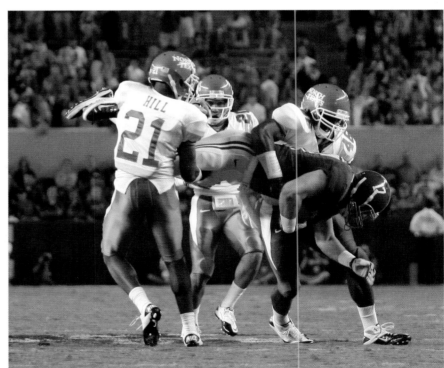

Josh Chapman and Jerrell Harris meet at the quarterback.

(Above) Barrett Jones prepares to block for Eddie Lacy. (Below) Marquis Maze on the run.

"THAT'S THE BIGGE... GETTING THE WIN TO OPEN UP CONFERENCE PLAY IS HUGE". - WILLIAM VLACHOS

GAME 4

SEPT 24

VS. ARKANSAS

— MARK BARRON - "WE WERE DEFINITELY READY TO GO. THEY TALKED A LOT COMING IN AND THAT ONLY MOTIVATED US SO TO COME OUT AND DO WHAT WE DID."

"IT WAS A GREAT TEAM WIN. WHEN I SAY TEAM WIN, I'M TALKING ABOUT ALL THE PLAYERS, ALL THE FANS, ALL THE PEOPLE IN THE ORGANIZATION WHO CONTRIBUTE TO THE SUCCESS OF THE TEAM IN EVERY WAY." - NICK SABAN

CHANGE THE GAME

GAME

4 SEPT. 24
2011

38
Alabama
Arkansas
14

TUSCALOOSA, AL... FOOTBALL TEAM DE... ...ARK... BEFORE A SOLD-OUT C... ...1,821 SA... BRYANT-DENNY STADIUM. ALABAMA JUNIO... BACK TRENT RICHARDSON RACKED UP 211 TO... ON THE DAY INCLUDING A TOUCHDOWN RE... WHILE SOPHOMORE QUARTERBACK AJ MC... FINISHED THE GAME 15-OF-20 FOR 200 YARDS A... TOUCHDOWN PASSES. SENIOR WIDE REC... MARQUIS MAZE ADDED AN 83-YARD PUNT RETUR... A SCORE IN ADDITION TO FIVE CATCHES FOR 40 YA... THE CRIMSON TIDE DEFENSE HELD THE ARKAN... OFFENSE TO 226 TOTAL YARDS, INCLUDING JUST... YARDS ON THE GROUND. ADDITIONALLY, ALABA... FORCED TWO RAZORBACKS TURNOVERS, INCLUDIN... 25-YARD INTERCEPTION RETURN FOR A TOUCHDOWN... SENIOR CORNERBACK DEQUAN MENZIE.

#2

#12

38

14

OFFENSE

75 JONES*

3 RICHARDSON*

*SEC PLAYER OF THE WEEK

SPECIAL TEAMS

11 GIBSON

4 MAZE

91 WATKINS

DEFENSE

4 BARRON

30 HIGHTOWER

21 KIRKPATRICK

WE LIVE IT.

Prior to Alabama's Southeastern Conference opener against Arkansas, the challenge from head coach Nick Saban to the Crimson Tide faithful came twice, with barrels loaded.

On his Thursday night radio show "Hey Coach" and again the next day at the "Nick@Noon" fundraising luncheon, Saban's directive was loud and clear — get noisy, stay noisy and never let up until the clock shows zero time left.

Mission accomplished. Noise from the Bryant-Denny Stadium crowd was off-the-charts loud, and Saban's team responded with a 38-14 dismantling of the Razorbacks.

"It was a great team win," Saban said. "When I say a 'team win,' I'm talking about all the players, all the fans, all the people in the organization who contribute to the success of the team in every way. The fans were great out there today. The atmosphere was great. I think it affected their offense a little bit."

Four eye-popping, explosive plays sparked Alabama's fifth straight victory over the Hogs.

After the Tide's first drive stalled, placekicker Cade Foster trotted on for a 54-yard field-goal attempt at the Arkansas 37-yard line. Foster set up in his kicking stance, then quickly shifted left. A.J. McCarron, the quarterback and holder, stood up and took the snap from Carson Tinker. McCarron rolled right and found a wide-open Michael Williams streaking down the left sideline. The throw and catch were perfect, giving Alabama an early 7-0 lead.

With Alabama clinging to a 10-7 lead late in the first half, cornerback DeQuan Menzie picked off Arkansas quarterback Tyler Wilson and raced in for a 25-yard score. Not only did the touchdown give the Tide a 17-7 lead, it gave the players — and the fans — a huge lift of emotion going into halftime.

Early in the third quarter, Alabama's Marquis Maze took an Arkansas punt and — weaving in and out of traffic reminiscent of Tide greats David Palmer and Javier Arenas — scored on an 83-yard return, the 10th longest in school history. Maze's spectacular run of beauty put Alabama up 24-7.

On the Tide's next offensive series, Trent Richardson caught a short screen pass just over the outstretched fingertips of an

(Right) Head coach Nick Saban lets an official know he didn't like a call in the Arkansas game.

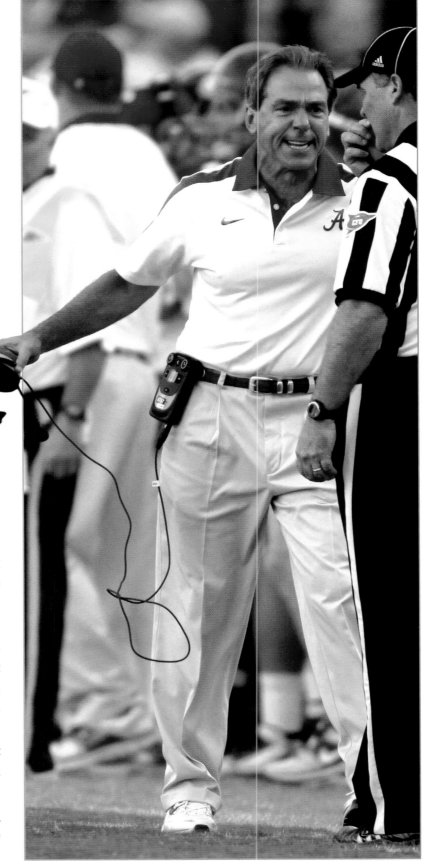

Arkansas defender and outran the Hog secondary for a 61-yard score, giving Alabama a comfortable 31-7 lead on its way to the 38-14 win.

While the Tide offense and special teams were clicking on all cylinders, the defense had an equally productive day, holding the potent Arkansas offense to 226 total yards, including just 17 yards on the ground. Led by linebacker Dont'a Hightower's nine stops, Alabama's defense notched 10 tackles for a loss.

Following the game, Arkansas head coach Bobby Petrino offered no excuses.

"They beat us in all three phases of the game," Petrino said. "They made big plays and we didn't. They hurt us with the fake field goal, the punt return for a touchdown, and the screen pass for a touchdown. We just couldn't get anything established today."

(Left) Michael Williams scores a touchdown. (Below) Dre Kirkpatrick holds on until help arrives.

Damion Square levels Arkansas quaterback Tyler Wilson.

(Top) Trent Richardson outruns a trio of Razorbacks.

(Above) DeQuan Menzie returns an interception.

Marquis Maze weaves his way in and out of traffic on an 83-yard punt return for a touchdown.

(Above) Defensive back Vinnie Sunseri celebrates a big play with linebackers Dont'a Hightower and Nico Johnson. (Right) The Crimson Tide conduct their postgame team prayer after the win over Arkansas.

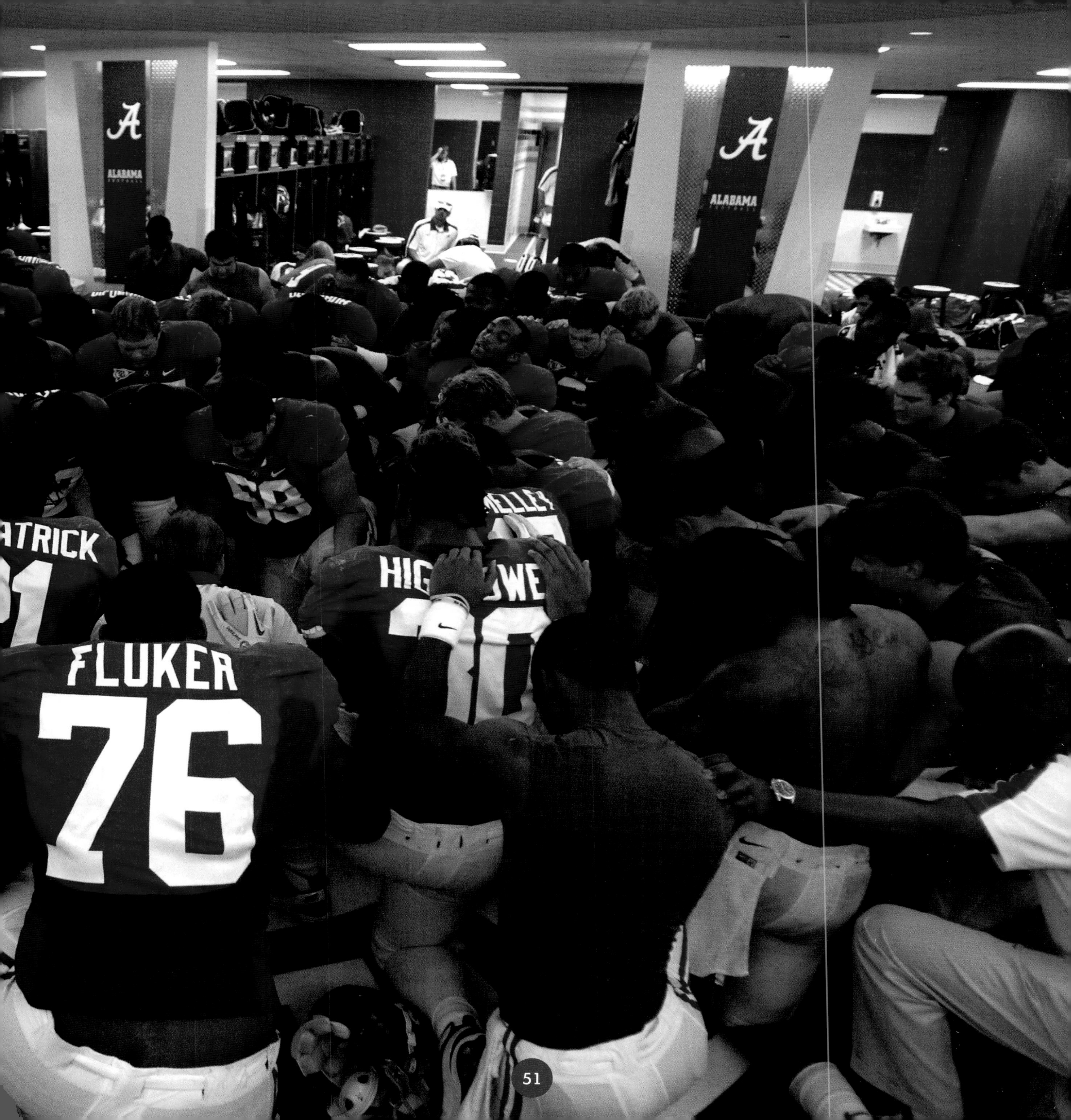
ALABAMA
ALABAMA
FLUKER
76

GATORAID

OCT1
VS. FLORIDA

GAME 5 OCT. 1 2011

GAME | 05 | RECA

GAINESVILLE, FLA - JUNIOR
TRENT RICHARDSON RUSHED FO
CARRIES, BOTH OF WHICH WE
THE NO. 3/2 ALABAMA G
DOWN NO. 12/12 FLORIDA
HILL GRIFFIN STADIUM
CRIMSON TIDE REMA
SEASON AT 5-0 OVERA NST SOUTH-

LEAGUE FOES. ALABAMA
FLORIDA TO 15 RUSHING YARDS FOR THE
244 YARDS SHY OF ITS SEASON AVERAGE.
DE COLLECTED 366 TOTAL YARDS OF
SE IN THE GAME COMPARED TO THE GATORS'
RDS. DURING HEAD COACH NICK SABAN'S
GAME TENURE, THE ALABAMA DEFENSE HAS
OW LIMITED ITS OPPONENTS TO LESS THAN 300
RDS OF TOTAL OFFENSE ON 34 OCCASIONS AND
AS NOT ALLOWED MORE THAN 251 YARDS THIS
EASON. WITH ITS PAIR OF TOUCHDOWNS IN THE
URTH QUARTER, THE TIDE HAS NOW OUTSCORED
OPPONENTS 45-8 THROUGHOUT THE FINAL
IN ADDITION TO OUTGAINING THE OPPOSI-
639 YARDS TO JUST 59 YARDS.

#2

38

#12

10

OFFENSE

SPECIAL TEAMS

DEFENSE

3	RICHARDSON**
73	VLACHOS
65	WARMACK

4	MAZE
17	SMELLEY
3	SUNSERI

| **41** | UPSHAW** |
| **91** | WATKINS |

*SEC PLAYER OF THE WEEK

**SEC HONORABLE MENTION

WE LIVE IT.

GAME 5 OCT. 1 2011

38
Alabama
Florida
10

"THAT IS SOMETHING WE P SELVES ON. I MEAN EVERY TIME WE HIT WE WANT TO HURT YOU. WE DON'T WANT TO END YOUR CAREER OR NOTHING, BUT WE WANT IT TO

"THERE ARE OBVIOUSLY A LOT OF THINGS WE CAN DO BETTER, BUT THIS IS ABOUT AS GOOD AS IT GETS FOR US TO BE ABLE TO COME

OUT ON THE ROAD AND GET... - NICK SABAN

If there is a "new school" rival for the University of Alabama football program, it is unquestionably the Florida Gators.

Until the famed 1992 SEC Championship Game in Birmingham's Legion Field, when Antonio Langham's fourth-quarter interception propelled the Tide over the Gators on the way to the eventual national championship, the Alabama-Florida rivalry was rather subdued, at best. In 24 games over a 75-year period, Alabama had won 16 and lost eight.

But from that 1992 classic to present day — thanks to Steve Spurrier's "Fun-and-Gun" offense during the 1990s and Urban Meyer's and Tim Tebow's fortunes in the mid- to late-2000s — the Gators narrowed the gap considerably, winning six of the last 13 games.

Unfortunately for Florida, though, the 2011 contest in the "Swamp" was not one of those victories.

A GAME THAT MATTERED:

In Dallas, 18th-ranked Arkansas defeats 14th-ranked Texas A&M 42-38.

(Below) Head coach Nick Saban gives a pep talk prior to taking the field against Florida in Gainesville. By halftime the Tide had served notice that it was a serious contender for the national title.

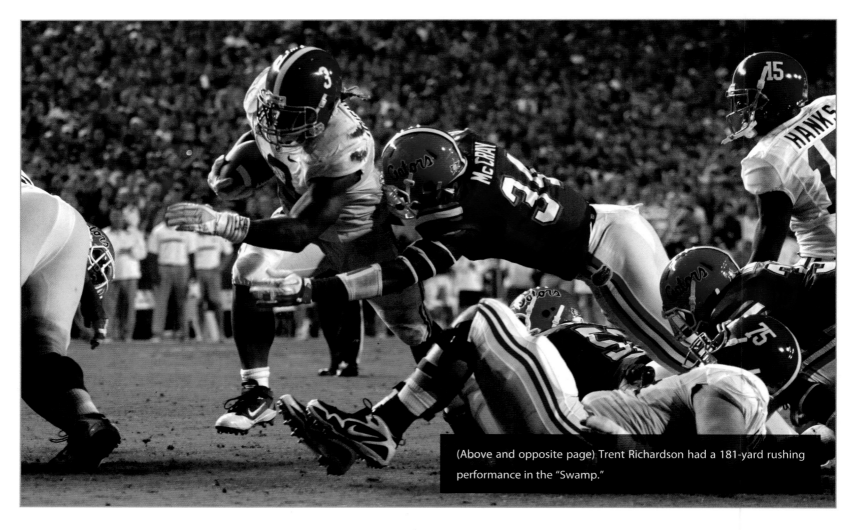

(Above and opposite page) Trent Richardson had a 181-yard rushing performance in the "Swamp."

After surprising the Tide with a 65-yard touchdown pass on the second play of the game, the Gators wilted from then on. Alabama, led by Trent Richardson's 181 rushing yards on 29 carries (both career highs) and a stout defense that allowed only 15 yards rushing, whipped the Gators 38-10, sucking out every bit of emotion from the rabid fans in orange and blue.

On a national prime-time CBS television stage and in front of the second-largest crowd in Gator history, the Tide served notice that it was a serious contender for the national title.

Courtney Upshaw, Alabama's do-it-all linebacker, was Florida quarterback John Brantley's worst nightmare. Early in the second quarter, Upshaw intercepted a Brantley pass and rumbled 45 yards for a score. Then just before halftime, the Alabama All-American knocked Brantley out of the game on a 10-yard sack, pushing the Gators out of makeable field-goal range. Upshaw finished the game with the one interception and four tackles, including three for losses of 21 yards.

"It was obviously a good win for our team," Alabama head coach Nick Saban said. "I think one of the most important things is when things didn't go well early, especially defensively, there was really no panic. In a tough environment, in a tough situation, I was really pleased with the way our team sort of competed through a lot of things that happened early.

"In boxing, you never know when you have a good fighter until the guy gets hit, gets staggered, and you see how he takes a punch."

Saban referred to, of course, his team's resiliency in absorbing Florida's quick-strike touchdown and answering with a dominative performance. The Gators, by contrast, were down for the count early.

For all practical purposes, the final bell rang on Florida by halftime.

(Below) After knocking Florida starting quarterback John Brantley out of the game in the first half, Alabama made things miserable for backup Jeff Driskel. (Bottom) Mark Barron, left, and Dont'a Hightower make sure the speedy Chris Rainey isn't going anywhere.

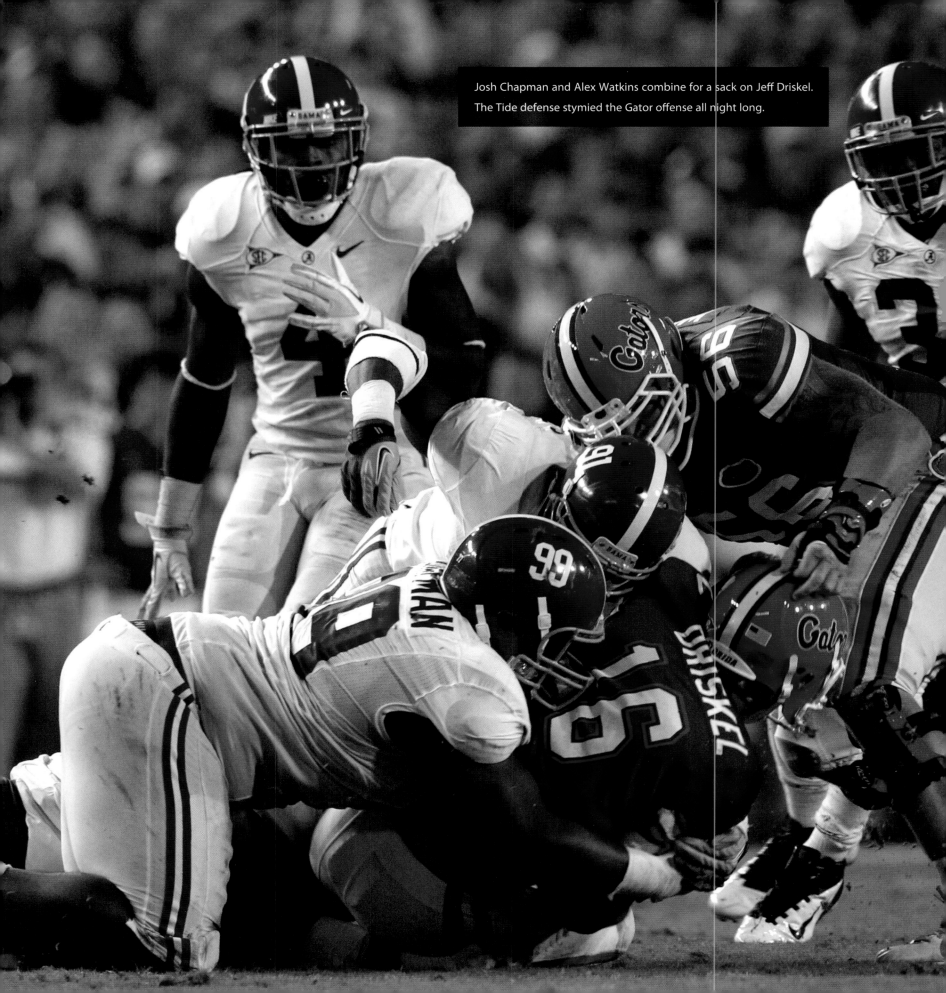

Josh Chapman and Alex Watkins combine for a sack on Jeff Driskel. The Tide defense stymied the Gator offense all night long.

Offensive lineman William Vlachos, who earned All-America Second Team honors after the season, thanks some Alabama fans who made the trip to Gainesville.

Florida head coach Will Muschamp shakes hands with Nick Saban after the Crimson Tide victory. Muschamp was an assistant under Saban at LSU and later with the NFL's Miami Dolphins.

GAME 6

OCT8

VS. VANDERBILT

RIGHT AT HOME

IN THE RED ZONE

GAME **06** RECAP

TUSCALOOSA, ALA. - SOPHOMORE QUARTERBACK AJ MCCARRON PASSED FOR 237 YARDS AND FOUR TOUCHDOWNS WHILE JUNIOR RUNNING BACK TRENT RICHARDSON RAN FOR 107 YARDS ON 19 CARRIES AND A TOUCHDOWN AS THE NO. 2 ALABAMA FOOTBALL TEAM DEFEATED THE VANDERBILT COMMODORES *34-0* ON SATURDAY AT BRYANT-DENNY STADIUM. THE CRIMSON TIDE IMPROVES TO 6-0 OVERALL (3-0 IN THE SEC) WHILE VANDERBILT FALLS TO 3-2 AND 0-2 VERSUS SEC OPPONENTS. THE SHUTOUT MARKS THE 28TH TIME THE ALABAMA DEFENSE HAS HELD AN OPPONENT TO TEN POINTS OR LESS UNDER SABAN AND IS THE SECOND TIME THE TIDE HAS SHUTOUT AN OPPONENT THIS YEAR. ALABAMA IS ALLOWING JUST 5.2 POINTS PER GAME AT HOME THIS SEASON

#2

OFFENSE

4 MAZE**
17 SMELLEY
89 WILLIAMS

SPECIAL TEAMS

43 FOSTE
24 MENZ

DEFENSE

4 BARRON**
30 HIGHTOWER

**SEC HONORABLE MENTION

WE LIVE IT.

GAME

6 OCT. 7 2011

3 4
Alabama
Vanderbilt

7

For the better part of a century, the Crimson Tide has enjoyed runaway success with homecoming games, winning 85 percent of them and giving the alumni something to celebrate.

From the first one in 1920 — a 21-0 Armistice Day victory over LSU (an eerily prophetic score) — to the 34-0 shutout of Vanderbilt in 2011, Alabama's 77 wins in 91 homecoming games have capped off colorful weeks of lawn decoration contests, bonfires, concerts and parades.

Although the final margin over the Commodores looked routine for an Alabama homecoming game, the victory was far from easy. Head coach Nick Saban called the game "a tale of two teams," referring to the Tide's first-half struggles against a gritty and improved Vandy squad.

"We didn't play very well in the first half," Saban said, referring to his team's 14-0 lead. "I think this is probably a pretty good example of how average you can be when you don't do things the way you need to do them — finish plays, finish blocks, make mental errors, don't tackle well. Most of that stuff comes from the mental intensity that you have going into the game, but I was really pleased with the way the team responded at halftime."

In the second half, the sold-out crowd of 101,821 saw a refocused Tide dominate the Commodores. After having allowed 142 yards in the first half, Alabama's defense held Vanderbilt to just 48 in the second. Moreover, Alabama had two interceptions and did not allow the Commodores to cross midfield after halftime.

Offensively, quarterback A.J. McCarron passed for 237 yards and four touchdowns, while Trent Richardson ran for 107 yards and a touchdown on 19 carries. It was his fifth consecutive 100-yard-plus rushing performance.

Alabama receivers also had a big day. Marquis Maze set a new career high with nine catches, totaling 93 yards, while freshman DeAndrew White contributed with three receptions for 58 yards and two touchdowns, also a career high.

McCarron's four touchdown passes versus the Commodores equaled his season total heading into the game, and were the second most ever in a game by an Alabama quarterback, joining Mike Shula (1985 vs. Memphis State) and John Parker Wilson (2007 vs. Arkansas) in this elite group.

Even in defeat, first-year Vanderbilt coach James Franklin was upbeat about his team and complimentary of Saban and the Tide program.

"I have a great amount of respect for Coach Saban and the job they've done here," Franklin said. "They recruit well, they coach hard and they have a great plan. That's their secret and that'll be our plan as well."

(Right) A.J. McCarron gets set to throw against the Vanderbilt defense, which he riddled for 237 yards and four touchdown passes.

(Top) Mark Barron prepares to tackle Vanderbilt quarterback Jordan Rodgers. (Above) Marquis Maze had a career-high nine receptions against Vandy for 93 yards.

Freshman DeAndrew White had a breakout game against the Commodores, catching three balls for 58 yards and two touchdowns.

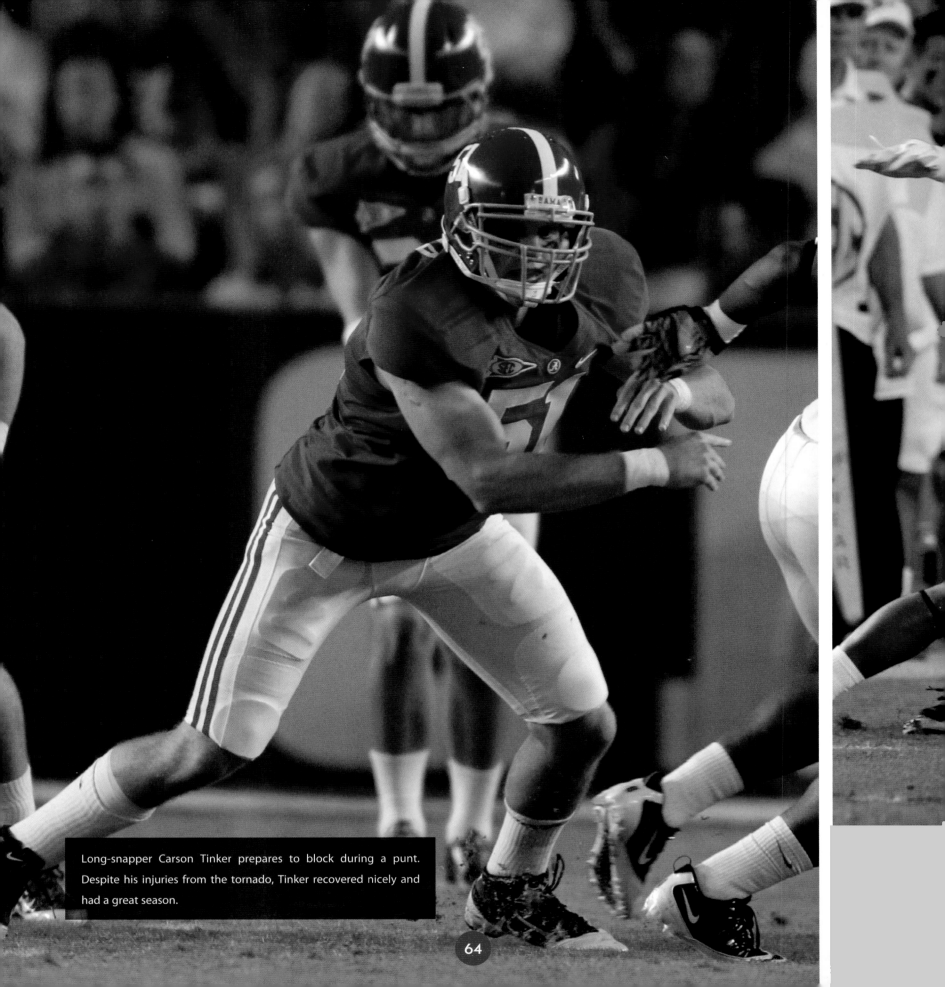

Long-snapper Carson Tinker prepares to block during a punt. Despite his injuries from the tornado, Tinker recovered nicely and had a great season.

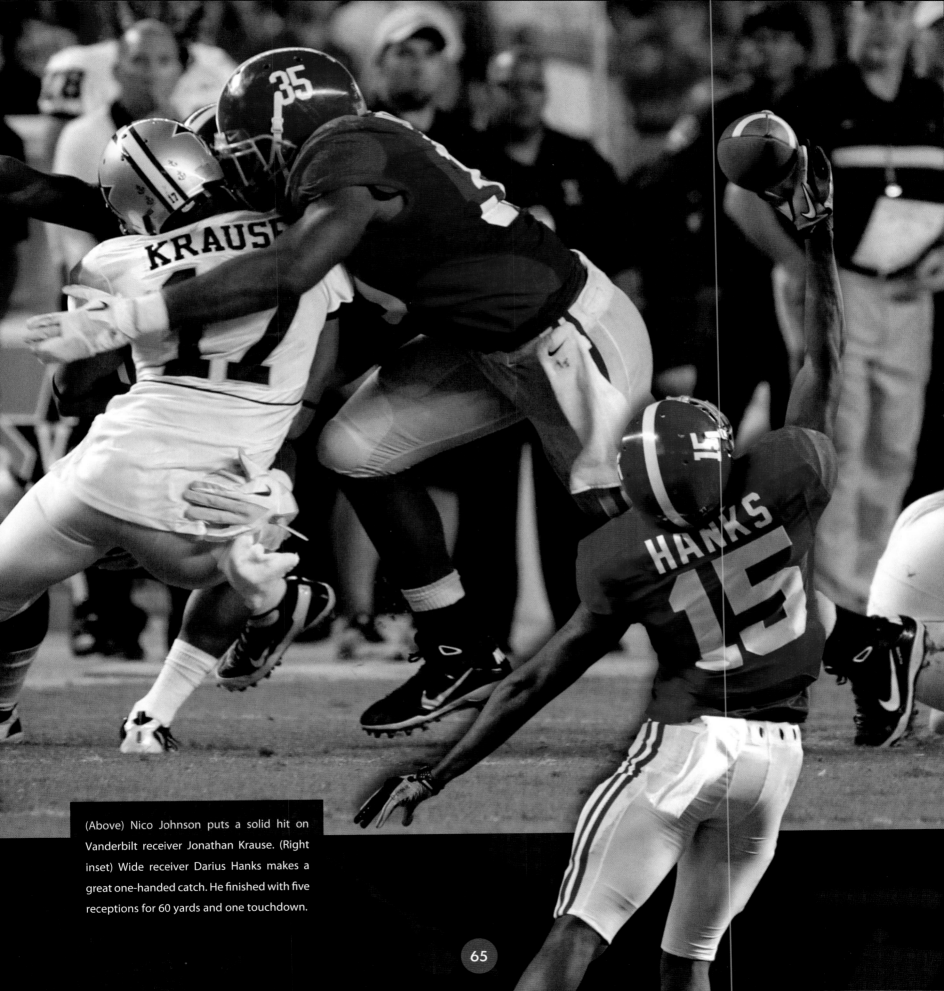

(Above) Nico Johnson puts a solid hit on Vanderbilt receiver Jonathan Krause. (Right inset) Wide receiver Darius Hanks makes a great one-handed catch. He finished with five receptions for 60 yards and one touchdown.

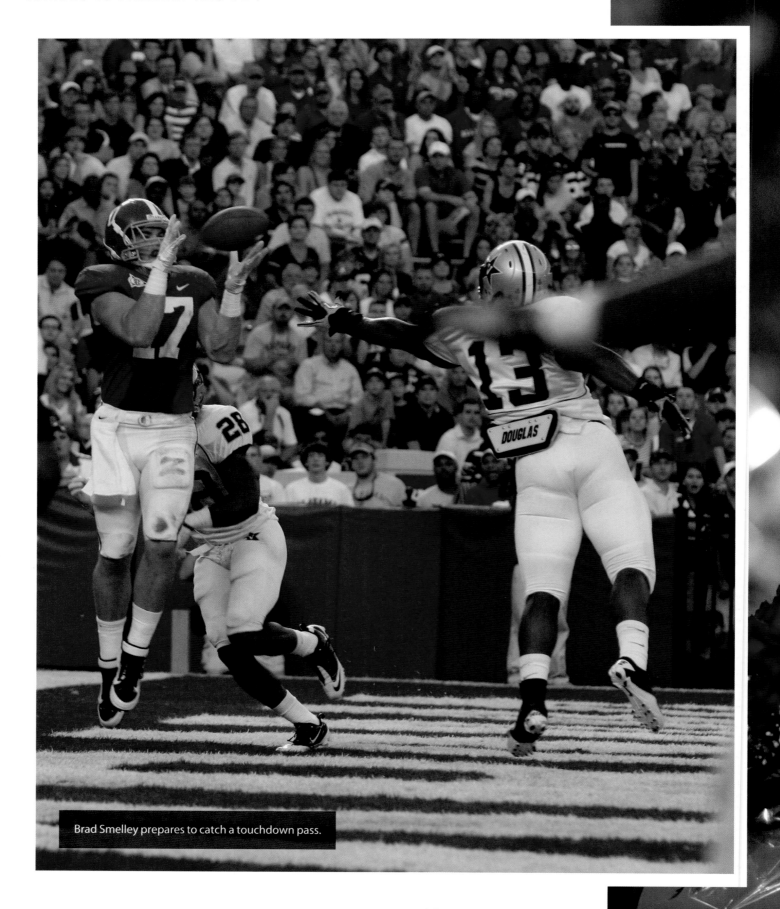

Brad Smelley prepares to catch a touchdown pass.

Homecoming queen Emily McLaughlin of Montgomery and her father, Jim, were in the spotlight at Bryant-Denny Stadium.

GAME

7 OCT. 15
2011

52
Alabama
Mississippi
7

UP FIELD AND I DIDN'T WANT THOSE GOOD BLOCKS GO TO WASTE." -TRENT RICHARDSON

GAME 7
Ole Miss
OCT **15**
VS. OLE MISS

RUNNING WILD

GAME **07** RECAP

OXFORD, MISS. - RUNNING BACK TRENT RICHARDSON RUSHED FOR A CAREER-HIGH 183 YARDS AND FOUR TOUCHDOWNS TO LEAD THE CRIMSON [TIDE] TO A CONVINCING 52-7 VICTORY [OVER] MISSISSIPPI ON SATURDAY BEFORE [A CROWD] OF 61,792 AT VAUGHT-HEMING[WAY] STADIUM. THE 52 POINTS SCORED BY [ALABAM]A IS THE MOST BY THE CRIMSON [TIDE IN] AN SEC GAME SINCE A 59-28 [WIN] OVER VANDERBILT ON SEPTEM[BER] 1990. RICHARDSON SCORED ON [RUNS] OF 8, 7, 8 AND 76 YARDS IN THE [GAME] WHILE MOVING INTO 10TH PLACE [ON THE] ALABAMA CAREER RUSHING [LIST] WITH 2,363 YARDS.

#2

52

7

OFFENSE

10 McCARRON
3 RICHARDSON*
65 WARMACK**

*SEC PLAYER OF THE WEEK

SPECIAL TEAMS

21 KIRKPATRICK
3 SUNSERI**

** SEC HONORABLE MENTION

DEFENSE

4 BARRON
35 JOHNSON

WE LIVE IT.

"THE LINE DID A GOOD JOB BLOCKING. THEY HAD A WALL FOR ME, THEN I JUST HAD TO MAKE A PLAY OUT OF IT WITH A FEW MORE GOOD BLOCKS

"WE'RE READY TO PLAY, WE PLAY PRETTY WELL," - NICK SABAN

"I THINK THERE'S ONE THING OUR PLAYERS HAVE LEARNED ABOUT [THE] PROGRAM OVER THE LAST THREE OR FOUR YEARS, THAT WHEN

L ook in most conventional dictionaries and the word "juke" is not there.

But take a peek into the "Urban Dictionary" and there it is: Juke - *to defeat an opponent by using subtlety, cleverness or trickery…*

Ole Miss freshman cornerback Senquez Golson didn't need the street slang dictionary to know what "juke" meant. He was a victim of it, first hand, compliments of Alabama running back Trent Richardson. The key definitions of the word —subtlety, cleverness, trickery — were all clearly on display.

Richardson's "The Juke" might not rank in Crimson Tide lore with "The Goal-Line Stand" (1979 Sugar Bowl) or "The Kick" (Van Tiffin vs. Auburn in 1985) but it'll sure give "The Sack" (Cornelius Bennett vs. Notre Dame in 1986) and "The Strip" (George Teague vs. Miami, 1993 Sugar Bowl) a run for their money.

Overshadowing Alabama's 52-7 blowout of the Rebels was the national buzz about Richardson's touchdown run, a 76-yard third-quarter scamper where he *twice* juked Golson, once 4 yards behind the line of scrimmage and again at about the 14-yard line. The latter was a jaw-dropping stop-and-go move that left the off-balance — and humbled — Golson frozen in his tracks.

"They (his Tide teammates) were telling me to give his ankles back, something like that," Richardson said after the game.

"The Juke" was one of four Richardson touchdown runs during his 183-yard performance. The Heisman Trophy candidate had plenty of offensive help, as Alabama's 52 points — highlighted by a 28-point third quarter — was the most by the Crimson Tide in a Southeastern Conference game since a 59-28 victory over Vanderbilt on Sept. 29, 1990. Joining Richardson in the touchdown department were Jalston Fowler with two and Brandon Gibson with one. Tide quarterback A.J. McCarron had an impressive night of passing, completing 19 of 24 attempts for 224 yards and one touchdown without throwing an interception.

(Right) Trent Richardson led Alabama's 52-7 stomping of Ole Miss by rushing for 183 yards and four touchdowns — including "The Juke."

After allowing a touchdown just 2:32 into the game, the Alabama defense limited the Rebels to 141 total yards the rest of the way. Linebacker Nico Johnson led the Tide with six tackles, including two for losses of 9 yards and had one quarterback sack for a 5-yard loss. Linebacker Courtney Upshaw had two sacks for 15 yards in losses and safety Robert Lester nabbed his first interception of the season, the ninth of his Alabama career.

Following the game, Ole Miss coach Houston Nutt lavished praise on the Tide's defense. "I thought going into this week they were in the top two or three that we've ever faced," Nutt said. "But after seeing them live, I think they're much better than seeing them on film."

(Below) Mark Barron prepares to make a tackle against Ole Miss. (Opposite page) Brandon Gibson hauls in an easy touchdown catch against the Rebels.

The Ole Miss offense had trouble against the tough Tide defense. (Above) Nico Johnson takes down Ole Miss running back Enrique Davis. (Opposite page) Courtney Upshaw, left, prepares to make a tackle while Ed Stinson draws near.

Wide receiver Kenny Bell gets upended by defensive back Charles Sawyer after a catch.

It was a happy Tide locker room after the victory. Ole Miss head coach Houston Nutt said of Alabama, "After seeing them live, I think they're much better than seeing them on film."

"SO IT JUST SHOWS WHEN WE HAVE INTENSITY AND FOCUS WE ARE A DANGEROUS TEAM, — NICO JOHNSON

UNRIVALED

IN THE SECOND HALF

GAME 08 REC

TUSCALOOSA, ALA -SOPHOMORE QUAR
AJ McCARRON PASSED FOR A CAREER-H
YARDS AND TWO TOUCHDOWNS AS
ALABAMA FOOTBALL TEAM DEFEAT
NESSEE VOLUNTEERS, 37-6, BEF
101,821 ON SATURDAY AT
STADIUM. THE CRIMSON TIDE IMP
OVERALL AND 4-0 IN SOUTHEAS
ENCE PLAY WHILE TENNESSEE
OVERALL AND 0-4 IN THE SEC. A
31 UNANSWERED POINTS IN THE
SEIZE CONTROL OF A GAME THA
6-6 AT THE HALF. JUNIOR RUNNIN
RICHARDSON TOTALED 110 YARDS (7
RECEIVING) ON THE DAY TO GO ALO
TOUCHDOWNS WHILE SENIOR RECE
MARQUIS MAZE ADDED 106 RECEIVING YARDS
FIVE CATCHES. THE CRIMSON TIDE DEFENSE
TENNESSEE TO JUST 155 TOTAL YARDS
FORCING TWO TURNOVERS. ALABAMA HE
VOLUNTEERS WITHOUT A FIRST DOWN
SECOND HALF.

#2

A
37

T
6

OFFENS

SPECIA EAMS

DEFENSE

4 MAZE	81 BUCK	TOWER*
52 McCULLOUGH**	43 FOSTE	35 JOHNSON
		41 UPSHAW

**SEC HONORABLE MENTION

*SEC PLAYER OF THE WEEK

WE LIVE IT.

"THE RECEIVERS WERE JUST ON POINT AND THEY JUST LET EVERYBODY KNOW THAT IT'S NOT ALL ABOUT THE RUNNING GAME. WE HAD A FULL TEAM OUT THERE." - TRENT RICHARDSON

"I THINK THE BIGGEST THING IS THE PLAYERS RESPONDED WITH A WHOLE DIFFERENT, SORT OF ENERGY LEVEL, PASSION, AND ENTHUSIASM IN THE SECOND HALF, WHICH MADE ALL THE DIFFERENCE IN THE WORLD." - NICK SABAN

GAME
8 OCT. 22
2011

37
Alabama
Tennessee
6

Wen it comes to playing the Crimson Tide, there must be something special about those teams from the state of Tennessee. Well, at least for half the game.

Only two games removed from Vanderbilt battling the Tide almost evenly for two quarters, another team from the Volunteer State — the University of Tennessee — outrushed, outhustled and outplayed Alabama in the first half, leaving the sold-out crowd at Bryant-Denny Stadium uneasy with the 6-6 score.

How quickly things changed, though.

After a spirited halftime challenge from head coach Nick Saban, Alabama responded like a champion, scoring 31 unanswered points to whip the Vols 37-6 and run its record to 8-0.

"Tennessee did a good job of kind of picking us a little bit in the first half and their defense played a lot of eight-man fronts," Saban said. "We threw the ball in the second half because it was really difficult to run it, and we were able to run it a little better after we loosened them up a little bit. We made some good half-time adjustments, and I think the biggest thing is the players responded with a whole different, sort of energy level, passion and enthusiasm in the second half, which made all the difference in the world."

Taking advantage of the Tennessee stacked defensive front, quarterback A.J. McCarron passed for a career-high 284 yards along with two touchdowns. Running back Trent Richardson totaled 110 yards (77 rushing, 33 receiving) and two touchdowns, while wide receiver Marquis Maze added 106 receiving yards on five catches.

The Crimson Tide defense held Tennessee to just 155 total yards, forced two turnovers and didn't allow a first down in the

(Below) Head coach Nick Saban leads his Crimson Tide out of the tunnel for the Tennessee game.

second half. Linebacker C.J. Mosley led Alabama with eight tackles while Courtney Upshaw added seven more, including a sack and a forced fumble. Freshman safety Vinnie Sunseri recovered a fumble in the fourth quarter, the first of his career, while linebacker Dont'a Hightower added seven tackles, three quarterback hurries, two pass breakups, a sack and a tackle for a loss to go along with an interception.

Saban noted the importance of the game and the Alabama-Tennessee rivalry, the second-oldest series in Crimson Tide history.

"This is a big game for our fans," Saban said. "I'm very, very happy that we were able to come out in the second half and win this game for a lot of people that this game means a lot to. It certainly means a lot to me. The crowd was great today, and they energized us in the second half, and that was really key for us."

As big a game as Tennessee was to Crimson Tide players and fans, nothing in Alabama football history could match what was about to happen two weeks later — after an open weekend — as top-ranked LSU rolled into Tuscaloosa.

A GAME THAT MATTERED:

In Norman, Okla., unranked Texas Tech upsets third-ranked Oklahoma 41-38.

Darius Hanks makes a tough catch, one of three receptions for 55 yards against the Vols.

A.J. McCarron unleashes a pass while Alfred McCullough and the rest of the offensive line does its job. McCarron finished 17 of 26 for 284 yards and one touchdown.

(Right) Trent Richardson battles a host of Vols for a few of his 77 rushing yards. Richardson also had two touchdowns. (Bottom) Dont'a Hightower and the Tide defense held UT to just 155 total yards and didn't allow a first down in the second half.

Marquis Maze had five receptions for 106 yards, including a 69-yard jaunt.

(Preceding page) Freshman defensive back Vinnie Sunseri celebrates the first fumble recovery of his collegiate career. (Below) It's always a joyous occasion in the Alabama locker room after a victory over Tennessee.

In crimson & white and purple & gold, toting barbecue grills and gumbo pots, yelling "Roll Tide" and "Geaux Tigers" until their throats were parched, they came.

From Thibodaux and Tuscumbia, Mandeville and Montgomery, Bossier City and Birmingham, they came.

With powerful traditions in tow and visions of No. 1 — and a BCS National Championship Game appearance — dancing in their collective heads, they came.

By the tens of thousands, they came for No. 1 LSU (8-0) and No. 2 Alabama (8-0) in the "Game of the Century" in Tuscaloosa, which on this day was the epicenter of the college football world.

Never before in the storied 83-year history of Bryant-Denny Stadium had an Alabama football game generated this much hoopla. Originally set for CBS Television's afternoon game, the kickoff was moved to the prime time 7 p.m. slot. ESPN's "GameDay" crew came early and stayed late, doing their best to convince the nation that two teams from the same conference — and same *division* — were the best in the country.

In an unusual defensive battle that saw two powerhouses slug it out in a mistakes-filled struggle, the Tigers prevailed 9-6 in overtime.

It just wasn't Alabama's night. Four missed field goals, including one in overtime, and two interceptions — including a freakish play at LSU's 1-yard line — were too much to overcome. Even then, the Tide had its chances.

Alabama's defensive unit played magnificently, holding LSU 30 points below its per-game average. Linebacker Nico Johnson led the charge with a career-high 11 tackles, while senior cornerback DeQuan Menzie had a career-high eight tackles. The Tide held LSU's offense to 222 total yards.

As usual, Alabama's star on offense was running back Trent Richardson, who totaled 192 yards on the night (89 rushing, 80 receiving and 23 on kickoff returns) on 29 touches. Quarterback A.J. McCarron threw for 199 yards on 16 of 28 passing, while wide receiver Marquis Maze hauled in a team-high six receptions

for 61 yards. Free safety Mark Barron and strong safety Robert Lester each added an interception for the Tide defense.

Following the game, Alabama head coach Nick Saban lavished praise on both squads.

"I'm really proud of the way our players competed in the game," Saban said. "I thought we played hard and physical and we played with a lot of toughness. It was a very physical game on both sides. We had a lot of opportunities in the game that we didn't take advantage of.

"These are two great teams. LSU has a very good team. They are No. 1 in the country for a reason. They played a heck of a game and our guys played a heck of a game."

Two postgame quotes — one from an Alabama player and one from an LSU player — spoke volumes about where each team would go from there.

(Above) Trent Richardson had a big night, finishing with 192 total yards on 29 touches, including kickoff returns. (Opposite page) Marquis Maze had six receptions for 61 yards against the Tigers.

"We still have a great opportunity in front of us," Tide center William Vlachos said. "LSU beat us tonight and at the same time we can't control our destiny, but we can control what we do from here on out. If we continue to keep the foot on the pedal and get better, I think we have a chance to do something very, very special this season."

When LSU safety Brandon Taylor was asked his thoughts on the game, he said, "Alabama's a tough team. They've got good players and an outstanding coach. I wouldn't want to play them again."

Quinton Dial wraps up LSU quarterback Jordan Jefferson. The defense held LSU to 30 points below its per-game average.

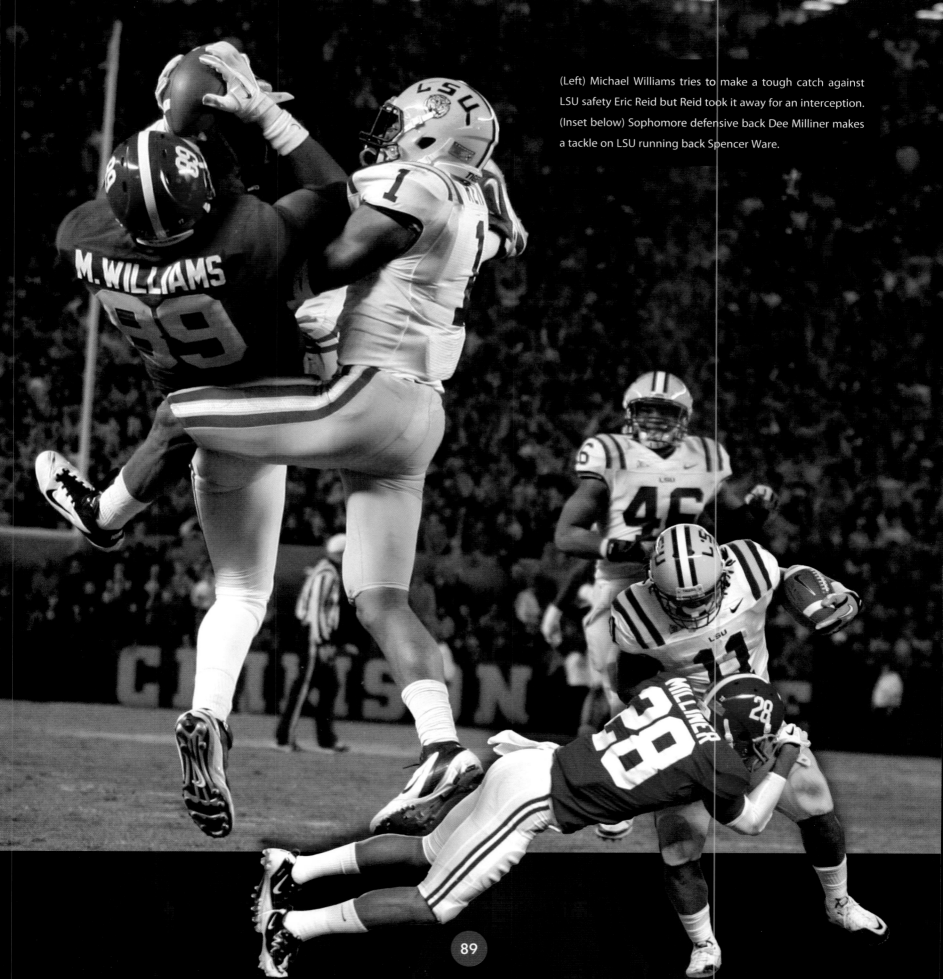

(Left) Michael Williams tries to make a tough catch against LSU safety Eric Reid but Reid took it away for an interception. (Inset below) Sophomore defensive back Dee Milliner makes a tackle on LSU running back Spencer Ware.

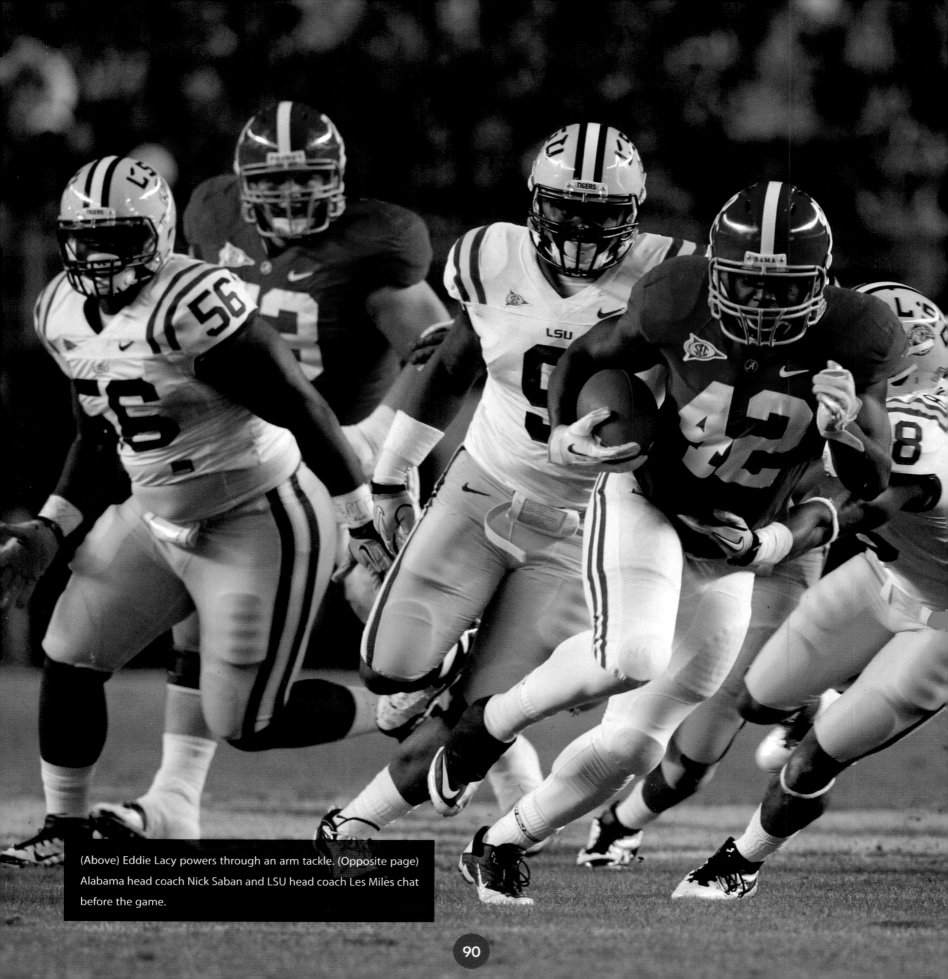

(Above) Eddie Lacy powers through an arm tackle. (Opposite page) Alabama head coach Nick Saban and LSU head coach Les Miles chat before the game.

M STATE

NOV 12
VS. MISSISSIPPI ST.

"I'VE GOT TO GIVE THEM CREDIT. THEY'RE OBVIOUSLY ONE OF THE TOP TWO TEAMS IN THE COUNTRY." - DAN MULLEN

"I KNOW THERE WAS SORT OF A *CHALLENGE* THAT PRESENTED ITSELF A WEEK AGO AND WE

RESPONDED

THE RIGHT WAY."

"I AM REALLY PROUD OF THE WAY WE PLAYED. WE HAVE TO PROVE WHO WE ARE." - NICK SABAN

GAME **10** RECAP

STARKVILLE, MISS-- THE ALABAMA CRIMSON
TIDE POSTED A 24-7 VICTORY ON SATURDAY
NIGHT OVER THE MISSISSIPPI STATE BULLDOGS
AT DAVIS WADE STADIUM TO MOVE TO
OVERALL AND 6-1 IN THE SOUTHEASTERN CON-
FERENCE, WHILE THE BULLDOGS DIP TO 5-5
THE SEASON AND 1-5 VERSUS LEAGUE FO
THE TIDE DEFENSE WAS LED BY JUNIOR L
BACKER DONT'A HIGHTOWER, WHO RECO
11 TOTAL TACKLES, INCLUDING THREE FOR
AND 1.5 SACKS FOR A LOSS OF NINE Y
SENIOR SAFETY MARK BARRONADDED
TOTAL TACKLES, FIVE OF WHICH WERE SO

#3

A

STATE M

24

7

GAME
10 NOV. 12
2011

24
Alabama
Mississippi St.
7

"I'M REALLY PLEASED AND PROUD OF THE WAY OUR PLAYERS PLAYED TONIGHT. I KNOW THERE WAS SORT OF A CHALLENGE THAT PRESENTED ITSELF A WEEK

OFFENSE

42 LACY
83 NORWOOD
3 RICHARDSON**
65 WARMACK

**SEC HONORABLE MENTION

SPECIAL TEAMS

31 JOHNSON
29 LOWERY
4 MAZE
24 MENZIE

DEFENSE

4 BARRON
30 HIGHTOWER*

*SEC PLAYER OF THE WEEK

WE HAVE A LOT OF THINGS TO IMPROVE ON. FROM A COMPETITIVE CHARACTER STANDPOINT I AM REALLY PROUD OF THE WAY WE PLAYED.

WE LIVE IT.

AGO AND WE RESPONDED THE RIGHT WAY." - NICK SABAN

After all the buildup, the hoopla, the craziness and the distractions of the "Game of the Century" — not to mention the heartbreaking loss — the Crimson Tide had no choice but to get off the mat and fight back.

If there was anything good that followed the loss to LSU, it was a surprise third-place spot in the ever-so-important BCS standings. The serendipitous news gave the Alabama nation hope that somehow, some way, the Tide could find its way back into the national championship hunt.

With this renewed sense of optimism, Alabama traveled to Starkville and silenced more than 50,000 cowbells and Mississippi State 24-7 in the process. The Tide's suffocating defense, led by linebacker Dont'a Hightower (11 tackles) and safety Mark Barron (nine tackles), held the Bulldogs to nine first downs and just 131 total yards. State's only touchdown came early in the fourth quarter following a 68-yard kickoff return.

A GAME THAT MATTERED:

In Stanford, Calif., seventh-ranked Oregon defeats fourth-ranked Stanford 53-30.

Mark Barron sacks Mississippi State quarterback Tyler Russell in Starkville. Barron finished with nine tackles.

Offensively, running back Trent Richardson logged the busiest game of his career, rushing 32 times for 127 yards, while Eddie Lacy rumbled for 96 yards and a pair of touchdowns.

After a shaky first half — including an interception that almost cost Alabama seven points — quarterback A.J. McCarron settled down and got the job done, finishing with 14 completions in 24 attempts to seven different receivers for 163 yards.

McCarron's gritty touchdown-saving tackle after the interception and an ensuing Alabama goal-line stand exemplified the makeup and determination of this Crimson Tide squad. Five plays after a first-and-goal from the 4-yard line (incomplete pass,

3-yard loss, false-start penalty, incomplete pass and missed 29-yard field goal), a dejected State offense trudged off the field, yet another victim to the nation's top-ranked defense.

In light of the previous week's loss to LSU, Alabama head coach Nick Saban praised his team for its resiliency in bouncing back against the Bulldogs.

"I'm really pleased and proud of how our players responded in this game," said Saban, who ran his true road game record to 15-2 since 2008 and 4-1 against the Bulldogs as Alabama head coach. "There was a challenge presented to them after the difficult circumstances of last week, and they responded."

MSU's Tyler Russell feels the heat as C.J. Mosley and Dont'a Hightower take aim.

Trent Richardson prepares to stiff-arm MSU's Wade Bonner. Richardson had 32 carries for 127 yards.

(Above) Eddie Lacy leaps for a few of his 96 yards against the Bulldogs. Lacy also scored two touchdowns. (Below) Sophomore wide receiver Kevin Norwood makes a catch.

Marquis Maze displays his open-field moves against State.

Quarterback A.J. McCarron explains a situation to head coach Nick Saban. McCarron completed 14 passes to seven different receivers for 163 yards.

A GAME THAT MATTERED:

In Boise, Idaho, unranked TCU defeats fifth-ranked Boise State 36-35.

Mississippi State quarterback Chris Relf has no place to throw as defensive lineman Damion Square wraps him up.

GAME 11

NOV 19

VS. GEORGIA SOUTHERN

FIN SH

GAME 11 RECAP

ON TOP

TUSCALOOSA, ALA. -- THE NO. 3-RANKED ALABAMA FOOTBALL TEAM DEFEATED THE GEORGIA SOUTHERN EAGLES, 45-21, BEFORE A SELLOUT CROWD OF 101,821 ON SENIOR DAY AT BRYANT-DENNY STADIUM. ALABAMA JUNIOR RUNNING BACK TRENT RICHARDSON RUSHED FOR 175 YARDS ON 32 CARRIES, SCORING THREE TOUCHDOWNS ON THE DAY, WHILE SOPHOMORE QUARTERBACK AJ MCCARRON THREW FOR 190 YARDS AND THREE TOUCHDOWNS, COMPLETING 14-OF-19 PASSES. SENIOR TIGHT END BRAD SMELLEY CAUGHT FOUR PASSES FOR A CAREER-HIGH 58 YARDS AND TWO TOUCHDOWNS FOR THE CRIMSON TIDE.

#3

45

21

OFFENSE

11	GIBSON
3	RICHARDSON
17	SMELLEY

SPECIAL TEAMS

30	HIGHTOWER
31	JOHNSON
3	SUNSERI

DEFENSE

| 4 | BARRON |

WE LIVE IT.

GAME
11 NOV. 19
2011

45
Alabama
Ga. Southern
21

The Alabama-Georgia Southern game, scheduled a week before the Iron Bowl, almost seemed an after-thought to the national media, judging by the over-whelming amount of attention given the BCS standings at the time.

But Tide head coach Nick Saban knew better. His answer to a pregame question about the Tide's chances of a rematch with LSU was swift and certain.

"I don't really care about that," Saban said. "I mean, I've been sitting in that room for two days watching film, trying to get enough guys on their pitch guy.

A GAME THAT MATTERED:

On the Friday night before Alabama's win over Georgia Southern, unranked Iowa State upset second-ranked Oklahoma State 37-31 in double overtime in Ames, Iowa.

Trent Richardson goes to the air to score a touchdown against Georgia Southern. He finished the day with 175 rushing yards and three touchdowns on 32 carries.

"You figure it out and come tell me what it is because I don't know. All I know is that we just need to take care of what we control, and what we control is how we play. My contribution to that is how we get the team ready to play."

That Georgia Southern "pitch guy" — quarterback Jaybo Shaw — and his teammates certainly proved Saban's concern worthy, rolling to 341 yards of offense against the vaunted Alabama defense. But it was the Tide that prevailed over the Eagles 45-21.

A GAME THAT MATTERED:
In Waco, Texas, No. 22 Baylor defeats No. 5 Oklahoma 45-38.

Defensive coordinator Kirby Smart reminds linebackers Courtney Upshaw, Jerrell Harris and Nico Johnson to keep their eyes on GSU "pitch guy" Jaybo Shaw.

A GAME THAT MATTERED:

In Eugene, Ore., Southern California defeats fourth-ranked Oregon 38-35.

Although Alabama had the game in hand from start to finish, it was not without its moments. Georgia Southern, a member of the Football Championship Subdivision (FCS) — formerly known as Division 1-AA — is an FCS power, having won six national championships. Its unique style of option offense gave the Tide fits, as evidenced by the final stats. Of the Eagles' 341 total yards, 302 were on the ground, the most all season by any Alabama opponent.

As usual, running back Trent Richardson starred for the Tide, rushing for 175 yards on 32 carries and scoring three touchdowns. Quarterback A.J. McCarron completed 14 of 19 passes for 190 yards and three touchdowns. Tight end Brad Smelley caught four passes for a career-high 58 yards and two touchdowns.

Safety Mark Barron led Alabama with eight tackles on the day. Quinton Dial also registered eight tackles, a career-high for the junior defensive lineman, while linebacker Nico Johnson and Dont'a Hightower each added six tackles.

Richardson's third-quarter touchdown run gave him 20 for the season, breaking former Tide great Shaun Alexander's mark of 19 set in 1999.

"It (the record) means a lot," Richardson said. "I didn't even know it until after the game. Records are meant to be broken.

"As a team — I never say 'I' — but as a team, we did break that record today."

(Right) A.J. McCarron had his way with the Georgia Southern defense, completing 14 of 19 passes for 190 yards and three touchdowns.

Marquis Maze on the run against the Eagles. Maze finished with three receptions for 44 yards.

Dont'a Hightower and his teammates get their hands up to block a 42-yard field-goal attempt by Adrian Mora.

(Above) Dre Kirkpatrick runs back the blocked field-goal attempt for 55 yards and a touchdown. (Above right) Offensive lineman William Vlachos discusses an assignment with coach Jeff Stoutland. (Right) Sophomore running back Jalston Fowler prepares to lower the boom on GSU linebacker Darius Eubanks. (Opposite page) Keepsake footballs are readied for the seniors on Senior Day.

"ANYTHING IT TAKES TO WIN. IF THAT'S WHAT IT TAKES TO WIN, I WILL DO IT." - TRENT RICHARDSON

GAME 12
AU
NOV 26
VS. AUBURN

GAME
12 NOV. 26 2011

RESTORE THE ORDER

#2 #24

12 RECAP

THE NO. 2 RANKED ALABAMA ... BEAT NO. 24 AUBURN, 42-14, IN ... STADIUM SATURDAY, GOING TO ... THE SEASON AND 7-1 IN SOUTHEASTERN ... WHILE THE TIGERS FELL TO ... THE CRIMSON TIDE FINISHED ... YARDS OF OFFENSE LED BY ... BACK TRENT RICHARDSON ... HIS WAY TO A CAREER ... CAUGHT A TOUCHDOWN ... TO MOVE WITHIN ONE ... TOUCHDOWN RECORD ... DEFENSIVELY, ALABAMA ... 140 YARDS OFFENSIVE ...

42 Alabama Auburn 14

42 14

OFFENSE

3 RICHARDSON* SEC
17 SMELLEY
73 VLACHOS* SEC

*SEC PLAYER OF THE WEEK

SPECIAL TEAMS

29 MANDELL
28 MILLINER
91 WATKINS

DEFENSE

30 HIGHTOWER
28 MILLINER
41 UPSHAW

WE LIVE IT.

"WE DEFINITELY HAD TO WIN THIS GAME. WE KNEW WHAT WAS AT STAKE. WE JUST HAD TO COME OUT AND PLAY OUR GAME AND THAT'S WHAT WE DID." - AJ McCARRON

"I'M REALLY PROUD OF THE EFFORT THAT THEY GAVE, AND ALL OF THE WORK THAT THEY HAVE DONE ALL YEAR LONG. OUR GOAL TODAY WAS TO PLAY OUR BEST FOOTBALL GAME, AND TO PLAY THE BEST THAT WE COULD PLAY." - NICK SABAN

For an entire year — from the time when Auburn rallied from 24 points down to defeat Alabama 28-27 in Tuscaloosa on the way to the 2010 national championship — the "Never Again" reminders were everywhere.

"Never Again" in the weight room. "Never Again" in the locker room. "Never Again" in the football offices. Most of the reminders came in the form of signs located throughout the Crimson Tide football facilities, but that didn't stop strength coach Scott Cochran from delivering his own "Never Again" screams at every workout, every day.

The resulting 42-14 thrashing of rival Auburn in Jordan-Hare Stadium sure helped take the sting away from the previous season's bitter defeat.

"I don't think there are really any words to describe how proud I am of our players and the people in our organization that have worked so hard this year," Alabama head coach Nick Saban

A.J. McCarron passes to a wide-open Michael Williams at Jordan-Hare Stadium. In his first Iron Bowl start, McCarron completed 18 of 23 pass attempts for 184 yards and three touchdowns.

said following the game. "I'm really proud of the effort they gave and all of the work they have done all year long. Our goal today was to play our best football game, and to play the best that we could play. I'm satisfied with what our players did."

In the Tide's victory, running back Trent Richardson powered his way to a career-best 203 rushing yards on 27 attempts, including a fourth-quarter 57-yarder full of stiff-arms and jaw-dropping jukes.

Quarterback A.J. McCarron put together a solid performance in his first Iron Bowl as a starter, going 18 for 23 with 184 yards and three touchdowns. His touchdown passes equaled an Alabama record against Auburn as he became the fourth Tide quarterback to throw three touchdown passes against the Tigers, joining Steve Sloan (1964), Jeff Rutledge (1978) and Freddie Kitchens (1996).

If there was an unsung hero in the Alabama offense's 397-yard output, it was senior tight end Brad Smelley, who had a career day in receptions (six) and yards (86) to lead the Tide in both categories. Smelley also scored a touchdown, his third in two games.

Defensively, Alabama held the Tigers to just 140 yards, with Auburn's touchdowns coming on a fumble recovery in the end zone and an 83-yard kickoff return. The Tigers' one-two running back punch of Michael Dyer and Onterio McCalebb could muster only a combined 54 yards.

Having remained fairly quiet since midseason about the BCS standings, Saban used the postgame press conference to brag on his Crimson Tide.

"I think we have a great football team, a great bunch of young men who have done a wonderful job, and they have played some really dominant football on both sides of the ball," Saban said. "I would be excited for our team if they had the opportunity to play for the national championship. I think they deserve it, and I think they have worked hard. They have all made a tremendous commitment."

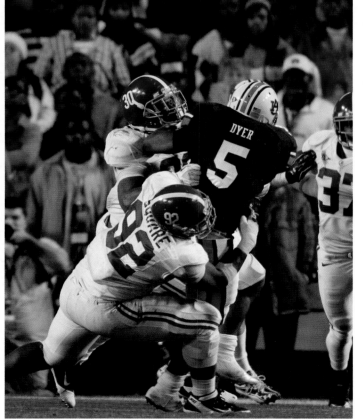

(Preceding page) Brad Smelley had a career day against Auburn, with six receptions for 86 yards and one touchdown. (Inset left) Damion Square and Dont'a Hightower take down Auburn running back Michael Dyer. The Alabama defense held the Tigers to 140 yards on offense.

(Below) Dee Milliner upends Auburn tight end Philip Lutzenkirchen. In the fourth quarter, Milliner picked off a pass and ran it back 35 yards for a touchdown. (Opposite page) C.J. Mosley gets his arms around Auburn's Kiehl Frazier.

(Below) Dre Kirkpatrick goes high to break up a pass intended for AU's Emory Blake. (Opposite page) Head coach Nick Saban acknowledges the Crimson Tide fans in Jordan-Hare Stadium after the 42-14 victory.

115

BCS NATIONAL CHAMPIONSHIP GAME

JAN. 9 2012

21 Alabama

LSU 0

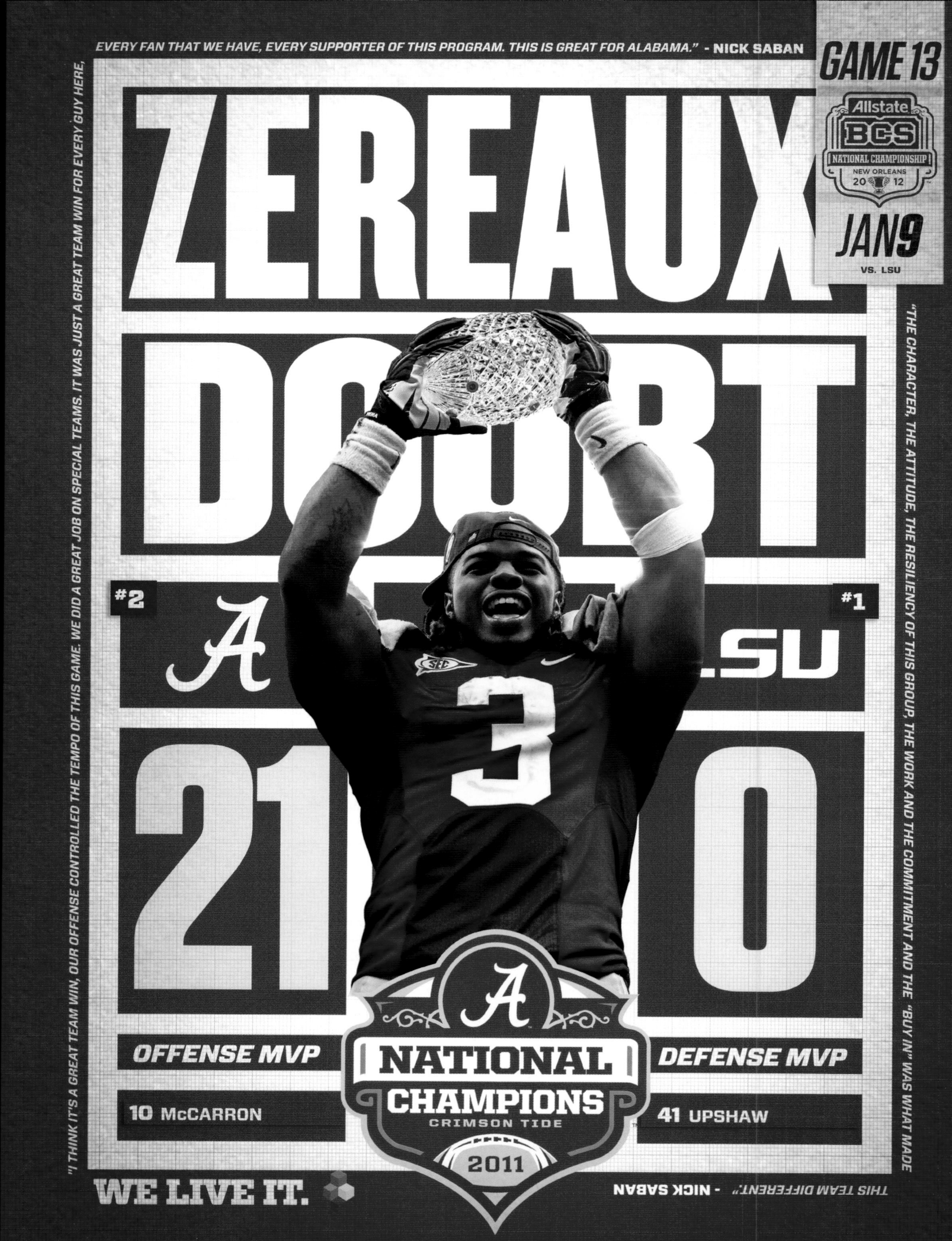

"I THINK IT'S A GREAT TEAM WIN, OUR OFFENSE CONTROLLED THE TEMPO OF THIS GAME. WE DID A GREAT JOB ON SPECIAL TEAMS. IT WAS JUST A GREAT TEAM WIN FOR EVERY GUY HERE, EVERY FAN THAT WE HAVE, EVERY SUPPORTER OF THIS PROGRAM. THIS IS GREAT FOR ALABAMA." - NICK SABAN
GAME 13
Allstate BCS NATIONAL CHAMPIONSHIP NEW ORLEANS 2012
JAN 9
VS. LSU
ZEREAUX DOUBT
#2
#1
LSU
21
0
3
OFFENSE MVP
10 McCARRON
DEFENSE MVP
41 UPSHAW
NATIONAL CHAMPIONS
CRIMSON TIDE
2011
WE LIVE IT.
"THE CHARACTER, THE ATTITUDE, THE RESILIENCY OF THIS GROUP, THE WORK AND THE COMMITMENT AND THE "BUY IN" WAS WHAT MADE THIS TEAM DIFFERENT." - NICK SABAN

Sign, sign, everywhere a sign
Blockin' out the scenery, breakin' my mind
Do this, don't do that, can't you read the sign?
— "Signs" by the Five Man Electrical Band, 1971

LSU head football coach Les Miles should have seen the sign.

No, not a big interstate highway overpass sign, but more like a bad omen that he and his LSU Tigers received as their team buses rolled toward New Orleans and a date in the 2012 BCS National Championship Game with the Alabama Crimson Tide.

Just as the LSU convoy was arriving in the city on Interstate 10 after the ride from Baton Rouge, the Alabama team buses merged from the airport ramp onto the highway at the exact same instant. With blue lights flashing and sirens wailing from both convoys, somebody — or something — had to give.

LSU blinked.

The Tigers' buses were forced to stop completely and wait as the Crimson Tide entourage moved ahead of them under police escort and on to their hotel. As events would later prove, Ala-

bama's victory on the interstate was just the first of what would become total domination over LSU in New Orleans, where the Tigers had previously won nine consecutive football games, including national championships in 2003 and 2007.

There would be no LSU celebrations this time. Alabama's 21-0 victory over the Tigers in the Mercedes-Benz Superdome was the first shutout in BCS title game history. It was also the culmination of a wild and crazy couple of months that saw the second-ranked Tide fall to No. 1 LSU 9-6 in Tuscaloosa on Nov. 5, then — with some help — climb its way back to the No. 2 spot in the BCS standings by a razor-thin margin.

In a remarkable "will-to-win" journey following the devastating Tuscaloosa tornado of April 27, this Alabama team solidified its spot as one of the all-time favorites in Crimson Tide lore. For eternity, those two events — the tornado and the Tide's 2011 national championship — are inseparably linked.

(Below) Head coach Nick Saban talks to his players before second-ranked Alabama takes the field against top-ranked LSU in the BCS National Championship Game in New Orleans.

(Below and opposite page) The Mercedes-Benz Superdome was the final destination for the 2011 Alabama team that had a "will to win" following the devastating tornado that hit Tuscaloosa on April 27. (Opposite page, far right) Lindsey Norris was there to cheer on her Crimson Tide.

GETTING TO THE DANCE

One doesn't have to be a math major to understand the complexities of the BCS voting process, but it helps. Created in 1998, the BCS was designed to end shared championships and to decide a winner on the field rather than at the ballot box. Using a combination of "human polls" (Harris Interactive Poll and USA Today Coaches Poll) and six different computer rankings, the BCS standings determine at season's end the participants in the BCS National Championship Game, as well as those in the Rose, Fiesta, Sugar and Orange bowls.

Going into the "Game of the Century" in Tuscaloosa on Nov. 5, undefeated LSU and Alabama were easily the top two teams in the BCS standings, with Oklahoma State a distant third. The day after LSU kicker Drew Alleman connected on a 25-yard field goal in overtime to defeat the Tide, the BCS crunched the numbers and released its new poll. Alabama — expected to fall to fourth behind LSU, Oklahoma State and Stanford — got a nice surprise with a third-place showing, giving the Tide hope for a trip to the title game.

From that point on, Alabama did its part, defeating Mississippi State, Georgia Southern and Auburn to finish 11-1. Along the way, several upsets aided the Tide (TCU over Boise State, Oregon over Stanford, Southern California over Oregon, and Baylor over Oklahoma), but none was more meaningful than unranked Iowa State's shocking double-overtime 37-31 win over No. 2 Oklahoma State in Ames, Iowa. The upset dropped the Cowboys to No. 4 while the Tide moved back up to the No. 2 spot. (Arkansas, a 38-14 victim to Alabama earlier in the season, moved up to No. 3, only the second time in poll history that three teams from the same conference held the top three spots).

Shortly after LSU disposed of Georgia on Dec. 3 in the SEC Championship Game, Oklahoma State turned some heads with a 44-10 trouncing of No. 9 Oklahoma. Many believed that the impressive showing by the Cowboys could vault them ahead of the Tide in the final BCS standings the next day.

For the next 18 hours, Alabama and Oklahoma State played the waiting game. For the Cowboys, their message to the voters was primarily that the Crimson Tide had already had its chance.

Oklahoma State head coach Mike Gundy even added to the furor when, after his team's rout of Oklahoma, he mentioned the first Alabama-LSU score in making a case for his team on ESPN:

(Above) Quarterback A.J. McCarron watches Trent Richardson (opposite page) make a cut behind his offensive line.

120

After avoiding LSU defensive tackle Anthony Johnson (56), running back Eddie Lacy puts a move on Ryan Baker, left, and Eric Reid.

"I think people have to decide if they want a 9-6 game or a 39-36 game. There is no question Oklahoma State should be No. 2. There's no question."

Yet, the Crimson Tide had a quiet but strong argument that its only loss was an overtime heartbreaker to the No. 1 team. The fact that Oklahoma State lost to an unranked opponent late in the season — when its fate was on the line — was also a major factor.

Late Sunday afternoon, Dec. 4, Alabama head coach Nick Saban received private word that the Tide had secured the No. 2 spot and would get its rematch with LSU. That night, at the year-end football banquet in Birmingham, players, parents and guests erupted with shouts and applause when ESPN's Rece Davis officially announced the LSU-Alabama pairing on the "BCS Selection Show" on television.

"It is a great opportunity to play a great LSU team that is undefeated that we had a great college football game with, maybe the greatest college football game of the season earlier in the year," Saban said following the official announcement. "We have a tremendous amount of respect for them. I really do think these are two great football teams and it will be a great football game."

In layman's terms, just how close was the final .0086 margin (Alabama's .9419 to Oklahoma State's .9333) in the final BCS regular-season standings?

Linebackers Trey DePriest and Dont'a Hightower celebrate a big defensive stop.

LSU quarterback Jordan Jefferson tries to figure out what hit him, and it was Alabama safety Mark Barron.

"It was close, but it wasn't so close that there was a lot of doubt for me personally, for someone who followed it so closely," said Brad Edwards, ESPN's BCS analyst and a 1994 Alabama graduate. "Let's put it in these terms. If you were looking at it like a batting race in baseball, it would be the equivalent of one guy winning the batting title with, say, a .332 average and the guy behind him finishing with, say, .329. It was close, but it wasn't so close that if the other guy had gotten a hit in his last at-bat, it would've put him over the top."

Edwards elaborated on his analogies with examples from racing and football.

"Or, it would've been like a NASCAR race where a guy wins by a car length, not by a photo-finish," he continued. "It wasn't so close that you're holding on in the final second. You would have been able to tell the winner with several seconds to go. But it still would've had you on the edge of your seat with a quarter-lap to go.

"To those LSU followers who think they got short-sheeted by the BCS...To those Oklahoma State honks who insist their team belonged here Monday night...To those Associated Press voters who said they would keep LSU atop their ballots even if the Tigers lost to Alabama...To all of them, I say, 'Are you nuts?'"

—Gene Wojciechowski of ESPN.com

"Using a football analogy, it would not have been like a last-second field goal to win the game. It would have been more like a three-point win where the other team has the ball last and you turn them over on downs at midfield. They never quite got into field-goal range, it was never quite to the point where they were on the verge of tying it or beating you, but they were close enough for you to worry about the possibility of it happening."

While the national pundits debated over the pros and cons of the BCS, the feeling was almost universal that the system had, indeed, produced the nation's two best teams, despite the fact that both were from the same conference.

"We are not going to apologize for being in the game," Saban said following the announcement. "Our players created this opportunity and they deserve it. That's the system, and according to the system, we should be there."

And "there" the Crimson Tide was on Jan. 5, rolling into New Orleans and blowing by the LSU motorcade, just like they would do on the Superdome field a few nights later.

THE "REMATCH OF THE CENTURY"

When it was all said and done, after the last words had been spoken on game night by the ESPN talking heads (peculiarly dressed in purple and gold), it was obvious to the nation who the best team in America was.

From Miami to Minneapolis, Chicago to Charlotte, San Antonio to San Bernardino, and Tuscaloosa to Baton Rouge, praise for Saban and his victorious Alabama squad was widespread. Reflecting on the Tide's victory, one thing was clear — Alabama was better prepared, better coached, in better condition and more serious about the task at hand.

The headlines told the story:

"Bayou Bleauxout" – *The Tuscaloosa News.*

"Tiger Drag: Tide Shuts Out Toothless Tigers" – *The New Orleans Times-Picayune.*

"21-Zereaux" – *The Birmingham News.*

A staunch defensive effort, combined with a record-setting night from kicker Jeremy Shelley, propelled the Tide to the 21-0 victory, its 14th national championship and second title in three years.

Alabama linebacker Courtney Upshaw earned Defensive Most Valuable Player honors after leading his team with seven total tackles, including six individual stops and a sack. Fellow linebacker Jerrell Harris added seven tackles and was a constant disruption to LSU's option plays. Alabama quarterback A.J. McCarron was named Offensive Most Valuable Player after throwing for 234 yards on 23 of 34 passing.

"We knew that he (McCarron) was going to have to play well because we knew we were going to throw the ball," Saban said. "He showed great leadership and poise in making good decisions."

Shelley tied an all-time bowl record with five made field goals and set an all-time bowl record with seven attempts. His five field goals gave the Tide a 15-0 lead after three quarters before Alabama running back Trent Richardson sealed the win with a 34-yard touchdown run with 4:36 left in the game. It was the only touchdown scored by either team in eight quarters and an overtime of football, spanning both games, a clear testament to the strength of both defenses.

Richardson, who finished third in the Heisman Trophy race, rushed for 96 yards on 20 carries.

Linebacker Dont'a Hightower strips the ball from Jordan Jefferson to force a fumble that Nick Gentry recovered.

Marquis Maze sets sail on a 49-yard punt return.

Wide receiver Kevin Norwood makes a tough grab over LSU cornerback Tyrann Mathieu. Norwood finished with four catches for 78 yards.

"I think it was a great team win," Saban said. "Our offense controlled the tempo of this game. We did a great job on special teams. It was just a great team win. This is great for Alabama."

The Tide claimed the victory with a methodical performance on both sides of the ball, posting 384 yards of total offense while holding the Tigers to just 92, the second fewest in a BCS title game. The previous low was 82 yards by Ohio State against Florida in the 2007 BCS championship. The Tide also had 21 first downs to just five for LSU.

The Tigers couldn't seem to get much going on offense, thanks mostly to Alabama's stellar defensive effort. Upon crossing midfield in the fourth quarter for the first time all game, the drive stalled and left LSU facing fourth-and-18 on the Alabama 40.

If there was one single play that characterized the Tide's defensive domination of the game, it was the next one when linebacker Dont'a Hightower sacked quarterback Jordan Jefferson, knocking the ball loose at the 50-yard line. Defensive lineman Nick Gentry fell on the fumble to end the drive and set the Ala-

bama offense up at midfield with 6:15 left in the contest. Four plays later, Richardson scored the game clincher.

"I give credit to our opponent," said LSU head coach Les Miles, who expected — and received —- what he labeled "big-boy football" from the Crimson Tide. "We think we had a great year. We think that this team had as quality a run as there is in this country. We accomplished a lot."

With the win, Saban became the first head coach to win three BCS national championships, winning one at LSU before claiming two at Alabama. "I'm really proud of the way our team competed in this game today," Saban said. "To have two teams as good as our two teams in the same division, in the same conference, is pretty unique. They were the only team that beat us. I'm really proud of what our players did in coming back and winning this game."

Brad Smelley tries to stay in bounds with Eric Reid in pursuit. The senior tight end had seven receptions for 39 yards.

THE DEFENSIVE GAME PLAN

Alabama defensive coordinator Kirby Smart's defensive philosophy is plain and simple: stop the run; be aggressive and relentless against the passer; defend the middle of the field; be productive on third-down defense; and force turnovers.

Against LSU, Smart's philosophy was textbook perfect.

Stop the run? Check (LSU finished with 39 net yards).

Be aggressive and relentless against the passer? Check (Jefferson was 11 of 17 for only 53 yards).

Defend the middle of the field? Check (Time and time again, the Alabama interior line stuffed everything LSU tried).

Be productive on third-down defense? Check (LSU was two of 12 on third downs).

Force turnovers? Check (Jefferson threw one interception and lost one fumble).

"Forget all the talk about this LSU team possibly being the greatest in the history of college football. Its offense got abused by a stingy, hard-hitting Alabama defense that will go down as one of college football's greatest. The Crimson Tide made the Tigers, who totaled 92 yards of total offense — the second-worst performance in a BCS game — look worse than the asphalt on Bourbon Street after Mardi Gras."

—Thayer Evans of FoxSports.com

To prepare for the BCS game, Smart had to look no further than the Nov. 5 loss to the Tigers to develop a game plan.

"For that first game, there was a little bit of debate on which quarterback would play," Smart said. "Jordan Jefferson was starting to play more prior to our game, but Jarrett Lee was considered their starter. After Lee threw those two interceptions against us, Jefferson came in.

"There are a lot of misnomers out there that we didn't prepare for Jefferson in that game, that we were surprised he played, and that we weren't ready for the option. That's really not the case. We didn't play the option very well in the game, but it wasn't because we didn't prepare for it.

"Everybody forgets that the previous two years, we played against Jefferson," Smart continued. "If you look at our game two years ago in Baton Rouge, he ran a lot of options. Three years ago when we beat them in Tuscaloosa, he ran a lot of option then. We knew he would come into the game and run some option. We just didn't defend it very well."

Following the Nov. 5 victory over the Tide, with Jefferson in full control, LSU easily won its next four games against Western Kentucky, Ole Miss, Arkansas and Georgia.

"Since our game with LSU, Jefferson had kind of taken over their offense," Smart said. "He was the team leader. He was who Les Miles had hung his hat on and it seemed that he was going to ride the guy out.

"That became obvious in the Georgia game, when they kept him in for the second half, despite them not getting a first down in the first half. So if you're going to make a change, that's probably the time to do it. But they didn't. We knew then that they were going to stick with him through thick and thin.

"So, knowing this, going into the BCS game we were going to work harder on the option and make sure we could stop it."

Two weekends after the LSU loss, on the night before the Alabama-Georgia Southern game, Iowa State's upset of No. 2 Oklahoma State paved the way for the Tide to earn another shot at LSU in the title game. Upon hearing that the Alabama players had celebrated the Oklahoma State loss at their team hotel, the Tide coaches — primarily Saban — sent a stern warning.

"I wasn't really watching the Oklahoma State game that Friday night," Smart said, "but my phone was blowing up with texts, saying it might happen, it might happen…and then it happened. The next morning, we had a staff meeting before our pre-game meal. A couple of the guys who do room check at the hotel told us that after the game the night before, our players were going nuts, coming out their rooms and high-fiving because they knew we were back in the mix, that we could now control our own destiny.

"Coach Saban got wind of that and in our staff meeting, he told us, 'Look, guys, this doesn't change anything. We must win all our games anyway. The problem is that every team who's had a chance to control their own destiny has lost because they were so elated that somebody else lost to put them in that position. Now, we're in that position. Do you think I should say something to the team?'

"Coach Saban doesn't speak to the team during the pre-game meal," Smart continued. "We always walk in, say a blessing, and sit down and eat — that's the protocol. So in our staff meeting, he decided he'd better talk to them.

"Plus, as if the Oklahoma State game wasn't a big enough distraction, we were dealing with trying to get our guys focused on

Trent Richardson battles for extra yardage.

LSU running back Kenny Hilliard has no place to go as Nico Johnson (35), Ed Stinson (49) and Josh Chapman (99) bring him down.

Georgia Southern," Smart said. "As coaches, we knew it would be real scary — the preparation, the focus, the lack of respect our players had for them. We all knew what a tough offense we had to defend.

"So, in what I think was a turning point in our season, Coach Saban came in and grabbed the bull by the horns and told the players that he heard about how excited they were the night before. Then he said, 'Look, nothing's changed — it's the same scenario. We've got to win the next game, we have to control our own destiny, or we'll be the victim of some other team's celebration.'

"It kind of grabbed everybody, refocused them. It re-centered everything," said Smart. "It was a good move on his part."

During the 43-day layoff between the Auburn game and the BCS game, the Alabama coaching staff gave the players every resource possible to defeat the Tigers, in terms of Xs and Os, tendencies, game plans, etc.

One thing the players didn't need to be taught, though, was motivation.

"I think our players knew from the first game that we were better than LSU," Smart said. "And for LSU to get the distinction of being such a great team, we felt like that was our role, especially defensively. There's no question that our kids felt like we were the best defense in the country, and the best defense — statistically — in the last 20 or 30 years. And they didn't like that fact that we had a blemish on our record.

"They were still upset that we didn't control the outcome of the first game better, things like penalties on the interception and LSU's field goal right before the half. Those might have been the difference in the game. And they didn't want those things to overshadow how great this defense was. And the only way to get that back was to win that game."

To prepare for the LSU offense, Saban, Smart and the defensive coaching staff hit the books — or in this case, the film room — to devise the defensive game plan. Despite LSU's offense

Jordan Jefferson had a tough night against the Tide. Sacking Jefferson on this play are Courtney Upshaw, Damion Square and Dont'a Hightower.

133

Linebacker Jerrell Harris (5) wraps up LSU running back Michael Ford.

being loaded with extraordinary talent from top to bottom, the final strategy was simple: stop Jordan Jefferson.

"The big thing for us was to control Jefferson and force him to throw the ball to beat us," Smart said. "We did a lot of studying and charting on his ability to throw the ball from the pocket, such as 'what's his completion percentage when he's throwing the ball between the two tackles?' We saw that it was not very high. His big plays came on scrambles, busted plays, or bootlegs when he got out of the pocket.

"But he did not have a lot of success throwing the ball in the pocket. We concluded that if we stop the run, including the option, and force him to throw the ball from the pocket, and not take chances up front and run out of our pass rush lanes or run inside and lose containment, control him, and make him throw the ball over the linemen and into small spaces, he won't be able to do it, and he won't be able to beat us."

The defensive game plan worked to perfection. The frustrated Jefferson was continually harassed by Alabama defenders.

"They (Alabama) were really prepared," said Jefferson, who fumbled three times (losing one), threw one interception, was sacked four times, completed 11 of 17 passes for 53 yards, and rushed 14 times for a net 15 yards. "They had a great defensive scheme. They did a great job shutting us down on the option. They did a great job on our third-and-short situations."

Reflecting back on the game and what — besides self-motivation — inspired the Tide to heights no one expected, Smart credits a talk to the team and staff from inspirational and motivational speaker Kevin Elko.

"It was absolutely amazing," Smart recalled. "Ever since Kevin Elko talked to us, there was such a confidence by the whole team. He did a great job of explaining the deal that the game was nothing more than a 'setup.' When he told them 'it's a setup,' every kid got that. They don't always get the analogies that our speakers make, but when Elko said 'it's a setup,' they understood.

"He basically took them back to the first LSU game and he went through how they felt in the locker room. He asked them to remember the taste in their mouth and the feeling they had.

"And everybody started remembering that feeling," Smart continued. "There were some upset and very emotional guys. And he said, 'Remember that feeling? It was just a setup. We set them up. Now they're trapped. Because they have to play us

again. And they already think they're better than you. It's just a setup.'

"And every kid was still saying that when they went out on the field prior to the game. 'It's just a setup, it's just a setup, it's just a setup,' they said. They bought into that.

"The whole redemption factor is always there," said Smart. "You go back to years of college football history and it's proven that it's hard to beat a team twice unless you're so much better than them. It's hard to do that. And you have an edge that they don't have. Elko just brought it out of them."

"Saban now has won three national championships, the most in the BCS era. He's now the unquestioned king of active college football coaches, and in Alabama lore, only Bear Bryant stands taller. (You can save the arguments on behalf of old-timers Wallace Wade and Frank Thomas.) If he sticks around a while longer, there probably will be more crystal footballs for the school's trophy case."

—-Pat Forde of Yahoo! Sports

Alabama players and coaches were confident they could beat LSU, but the shutout surprised many, even Smart.

"I had a strange, quiet confidence going into the game," Smart said. "The night before the game, I dreamed that we won 24-7. So for me to think that we would shut them out, probably not — not in today's day and age and not with the skill players they had. You would think they would make a play to at least score some points."

Smart credits superhuman effort by his defensive leaders — and lessons learned from the Georgia Southern game — in shutting down LSU's offense.

"People sometimes talk about a team or a player going through the motions, then flipping some kind of switch and playing great," he said. "But that week, Dont'a (Hightower), Mark (Barron) and Courtney (Upshaw) really took over that defense. And there was no doubt in my mind that those three kids were going to play the best game of their lives because of the way they prepared. They just had the look in their eye. There was no doubt they were hungry for that game. And that's what they did — they dominated the game.

"I'm not sure, secretly and quietly, that the Georgia Southern game wasn't a blessing in disguise for us for two reasons," Smart continued. "First, LSU watched it and tried to copy some of it.

But they can't simulate what Georgia Southern does. Georgia Southern has a doctorate in running the option. LSU has a high school degree in running the option. So to me, to copycat those guys was a mistake.

"And second, it also gave us another week to practice against somebody really good and replicate it all week. We didn't defend it very well, but the fact that we practiced it so much got us better for the LSU game.

"That Georgia Southern game could have cost us our 14th national championship because in theory we could've lost that game," Smart said. "With us playing poorly, they were good enough to beat us. So, you could argue that that game should have never been scheduled and we should've gotten out of it. But in the end, it secretly and quietly may have won the BCS game for us."

Statistically, the 2011 Alabama defensive unit finished the season not only as one of the best in Crimson Tide annals, but as one of the finest in college football history, finishing first in the nation in total defense, pass efficiency, scoring defense, rushing defense and pass defense.

Smart recognizes this group's role in history.

"It's hard to argue statistically with what this defense did," he said. "You take from the BCS era until now and I don't think you'll find a defense that was even close statistically to this one. Obviously in Alabama's history and college football history there are some very comparable defenses.

"But since the offensive takeover of spreads and scoring points, nobody's been able to do what we were able to do. I think that's a tribute to a good defensive philosophy, but more to the fact that we had five or six really good players."

THE OFFENSIVE GAME PLAN

Before Alabama offensive coordinator Jim McElwain became the former Alabama offensive coordinator, he had one last assignment to bolster his already stellar resume — devise a game plan to move the ball on the powerful LSU defense, ranked second nationally in yards and points allowed.

McElwain, who was hired as Colorado State's head coach on Dec. 13, wore two hats during Alabama's preparation for LSU. His biggest hat, though, was getting ready for the Tigers.

"Coach Saban was great in allowing me to do some things for my Colorado State job, but those things were done maybe early in the morning or late at night," McElwain said. "My priority was Alabama and getting our offense ready to play LSU."

McElwain's philosophy, like Kirby Smart's, is plain and simple — get the football into the hands of explosive playmakers; commit no turnovers; be conscious of field position; and be sound in all phases of offense.

Another word for "sound in all phases of offense" would be "balanced." The Tide was the only SEC team in 2011 to average at least 200 yards rushing and 200 or more yards passing. Despite the two slugfests with LSU, Alabama averaged almost 35 points per game in 2011 — led by Richardson, the Tide's single-season rushing leader and Doak Walker Award winner, along with quarterback McCarron and an offensive line anchored by Outland Trophy winner Barrett Jones (whose pre-game comment about the Tide "restoring order" was eerily prophetic).

That's why the Nov. 5 game, when the Tide scored only six points on two field goals, was such a motivating factor going into the BCS game.

"In the first LSU game, we shot ourselves in the foot with unforced errors — uncharacteristic penalties, illegal procedure, and we put ourselves in several bad situations," McElwain said. "When we went back and looked at the film, we saw that we stopped ourselves more than LSU beat us.

"It sure was a disappointment, but at the same time you compete and get back up and try to get better the next week," he continued. "And I think we did that. I think we got better throughout the season, especially with A.J. and the way he matured in his role as quarterback."

McElwain praised Saban for the way he set the schedule during Alabama's 43-day layoff.

"With that kind of break, the one thing you could do is spend too much time on the game," McElwain said. "I thought Coach Saban did a great job of setting the schedule — how our guys were going to work out, how we had a couple days of practice that was almost like spring ball, our breaks for the holidays, and how we practiced with no real focus on LSU, just on ourselves to get better.

"Then, when we worked in the game plan, we were set and focused with a real sense of unfinished business. Our guys were really into it.

"They realized they had gotten a second chance and they weren't going to mess this one up," McElwain continued.

Linebacker C.J. Mosley tries to avoid Jordan Jefferson after intercepting one of his passes.

"That's how they approached the practices and that's how they approached the week in New Orleans. I was really proud about how they took to the game plan and the task at hand and really did a good job of preparation.

"If we needed to get those guys motivated for that type of game, then something's wrong. If anything, it was probably in reverse a little bit, to make sure we focused on the task at hand, not let emotions run rampant, and be focused on what we needed to do. They were very confident going into the game."

Alabama's domination of the Tigers began at the coin toss and ended when the clock hit zero.

The Tide won the toss, deferred to the second half, and after holding LSU to 6 yards in three plays on its first possession, the offense wasted no time letting LSU know that things would be different this time around.

On Alabama's first possession, with the LSU defense keying on Richardson, McCarron threw three times for 25 yards to two different receivers. The seven-play, 36-yard drive stalled, but McElwain's game plan — throwing short passes on first down — moved the chains all night and kept the Tigers on their heels.

"The main thing we did different from the first game was some formational things — shifts and motions — where we tried to take (LSU All-American cornerback) Morris Claiborne kind of out of the game so he would end up in coverage a lot of times on the third tight end or the running back split out," McElwain said. "And, although Trent was our workhorse, we wanted LSU to know where he was at all times and wonder where the other guys were.

"Along with that, we wanted to get the Honey Badger (Tyrann Mathieu) in some one-on-one matchups. Where he really affects a game is as a blitzer. We tried to make sure we did some things from a formation standpoint to put him in some coverage situations."

McElwain lavished praise on McCarron.

"A.J. stepped up and answered the bell," McElwain said. "We knew we were going to have to make some plays downfield and he had a great grasp of the plan. I thought he did a real good job

(Above) A.J. McCarron played very well on the big stage, completing 23 of 34 passes for 234 yards. He was named the game's Offensive Most Valuable Player.

Mark Barron (4), Jesse Williams (54), Damion Square (92) and Robert Lester (37) gang-tackle Michael Ford.

of taking what the defense gave him. I don't think he forced anything. He knew the plan inside and out. He was aware of what they were going to do."

The unsung heroes of Alabama's victory were the receivers, especially after Marquis Maze went out with a pulled hamstring in the first quarter. Brad Smelley (seven catches for 39 yards), Darius Hanks (five for 58), Kevin Norwood (four for 78, including a breathtaking, leaping 26-yarder over Mathieu), Chris Underwood (two for 12), Michael Williams (two for 10) and Kenny Bell (one for 26) played the games of their lives.

"The receivers answered in their own minds that they had to go compete and I was really proud of how they did it," McElwain said. "I was real excited about the energy they came to the game with, as well as the focus on stepping up and making some plays. And they did that."

McElwain's goal of becoming a head coach is now a reality, but he'll always cherish his time with the Crimson Tide.

"I just told all those guys 'thanks' after the game," McElwain said. "A lot of them had been with me all four years I was there and obviously gave me everything they had for four years and 48 wins. I was proud of them and happy for them to accomplish what they did. Winning two national championships — now that's something.

"I can't say enough about how much I care for them."

"RED TAILS" AND REMEMBRANCES

Following the game, after the crimson and white confetti had rained downed upon the Tide players and echoes of "Rammer Jammer" finally disappeared from the Superdome, Saban could finally — and deservingly — take a breath.

In his postgame remarks, Saban said coaching this team was "a privilege." He likened their performance to the George Lucas film "Red Tails," the story of the World War II Tuskegee Airmen, which he and his players watched together a night earlier.

"Those guys' (in "Red Tails") motto was the last plane, the last bullet, the last man, the last minute, we fight," Saban said. "And I think that kind of described the spirit of that group extremely well, but it also describes the spirit of the group of players that we have on our team this year and how it took a tremendous amount of resiliency to come back."

(Preceding page) Vinnie Sunseri celebrates a big play. Vinnie Sunseri (3), Ha Ha Clinton-Dix (6), Alex Watkins (91), Xzavier Dickson (47), Jarrick Williams (20) and Trey DePriest (33) get in on the action.

Trent Richardson races down the sideline on a 34-yard touchdown run late in the game. Richardson finished with 96 rushing yards on 20 carries and caught two passes for 11 yards.

Saban's comments referred to the Tide's resolve in overcoming the painful 9-6 loss to LSU on Nov. 5, but could just as well have included the team's positive response to the devastating April 27 tornado.

At Alabama's national championship celebration back home at Bryant-Denny Stadium on Jan. 21, Saban wasted no time in praising both his team and the thousands who pitched in to help victims of the tornado.

"This team reflected the spirit of the people of the state of Alabama in the way they overcame adversity that was created by the terrible tragedy in the spring with the tornado," he said. "I can't be proud enough of them winning the Disney Spirit Award and the way this team represented the spirit of the people of our state, who had so much to overcome.

"Even though we're here to celebrate a 14th national championship, we really want to continue to rebuild our community and continue to represent the character of the people of our state with the competitive spirit we play and represent them with."

Nearly three months later, during the Crimson Tide's April 19 visit to the White House, President Barack Obama echoed Saban's comments in applauding the team's accomplishments on and off the field.

"This was a fun season to watch, but it was also a deeply meaningful season for the Tide," said Obama, who had witnessed the destruction in Tuscaloosa during a visit two days after the storm. "And what's even more impressive is that these young men showed that success isn't about the individual — it's about the ability to work as a team.

"They played as a team because of what they had endured as a team. And so each victory was about more than getting to the title game — it was about the lives of these players and coaches that they'd carried with them and what they meant to each other."

Wide receiver Kenny Bell takes off on a 26-yard gain.

(Below) When the clock struck 0:00, the national champions flag came out, signifying Alabama's 14th national title. (Opposite page) Head coach Nick Saban congratulates quarterback A.J. McCarron.

perdome

(Preceding page) Nick Saban never saw the Gatorade bath coming. (Above)
Dont'a Hightower shares a laugh with Coach Saban after his drenching.

(Below and opposite page) Nick Saban holds up the crystal football portion of the national championship trophy as his players celebrate.

HOW DO YOU WANT TO FINISH?

-NICK SABAN

(Opposite page) ESPN's John Saunders interviews Coach Saban. (Below) Trent Richardson has his moment with the crystal football while Brandon Gibson lets everyone know who is No. 1.

Alabama Athletic Director Mal Moore congratulates A.J. McCarron.

Alabama offensive line coach Jeff Stoutland, center, celebrates the national championship with, left to right, offensive linemen D.J. Fluker, Anthony Steen, Alfred McCullough, William Vlachos, Chance Warmack and Barrett Jones.

After the team returned to Tuscaloosa, it enjoyed a confetti-filled celebration at Bryant-Denny Stadium.

(Below) The team was honored by President Barack Obama at the White House on April 19, 2012.

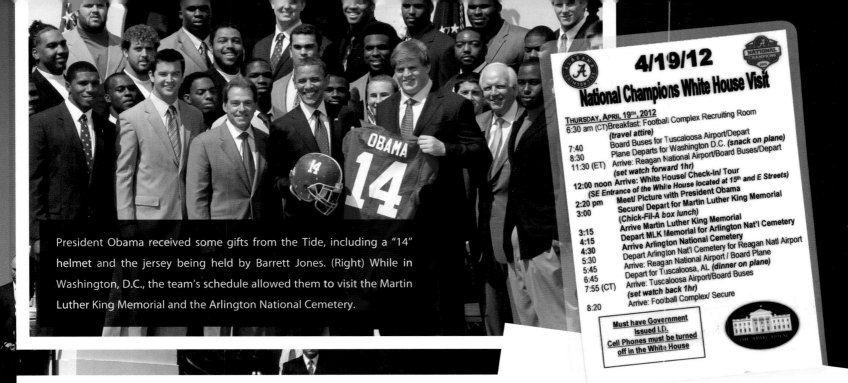

4/19/12
National Champions White House Visit

THURSDAY, APRIL 19TH, 2012

6:30 am (CT)	Breakfast: Football Complex Recruiting Room *(travel attire)*
7:40	Board Buses for Tuscaloosa Airport/Depart
8:30	Plane Departs for Washington D.C. *(snack on plane)*
11:30 (ET)	Arrive: Reagan National Airport/Board Buses/Depart *(set watch forward 1hr)*
12:00 noon	Arrive: White House/ Check-In/ Tour *(SE Entrance of the White House located at 15th and E Streets)*
	Meet/ Picture with President Obama
2:20 pm	Secure/ Depart for Martin Luther King Memorial
3:00	*(Chick-Fil-A box lunch)*
	Arrive Martin Luther King Memorial
3:15	Depart MLK Memorial for Arlington Nat'l Cemetery
4:15	Arrive Arlington National Cemetery
4:30	Depart Arlington Nat'l Cemetery for Reagan Natl Airport
5:30	Arrive: Reagan National Airport / Board Plane
5:45	Depart for Tuscaloosa, AL *(dinner on plane)*
6:45	Arrive: Tuscaloosa Airport/Board Buses *(set watch back 1hr)*
7:55 (CT)	
8:20	Arrive: Football Complex/ Secure

Must have Government Issued I.D.
Cell Phones must be turned off in the White House

President Obama received some gifts from the Tide, including a "14" helmet and the jersey being held by Barrett Jones. (Right) While in Washington, D.C., the team's schedule allowed them to visit the Martin Luther King Memorial and the Arlington National Cemetery.

Coach Saban talks to his players inside the White House. (Right) President Obama sent a letter to Coach Saban, thanking him and the players for the gifts, and acknowledging the trying times that had to be overcome after the 2011 tornado.

THE WHITE HOUSE
WASHINGTON

June 6, 2012

Mr. Nick Saban
The University of Alabama
323 Paul W. Bryant Drive
Tuscaloosa, Alabama 35487

Dear Coach Saban:

This is just a quick note to thank you for the kind gifts you gave me during your visit to the White House. I appreciate your generosity.

In trying times, the Alabama Crimson Tide embodied the strength, resilience, and compassion of the Tuscaloosa community. It was a pleasure to congratulate you on a well-earned victory and reflect on a deeply meaningful season.

Thank you, again, for your thoughtful gifts. I wish you all the best in the coming year.

Sincerely,

Barack Obama

Terry and Nick Saban enjoy a moment in the White House.

2011

Alabama Football Honors and Awards

ESPN.com's All-America Team (First Team)
Pro Football Weekly All-America Team (First Team)
CBSSports.com All-America Team (First Team)
Yahoo! Sports All-America Team (First Team)
First-Team All-SEC (Coaches and AP)

DONT'A HIGHTOWER
Team Captain
Consensus First-Team All-American
AP All-America Team (First Team)
Walter Camp All-America Team (First Team)
AFCA FBS Coaches' All-America Team (First Team)
Pro Football Weekly All-America Team (First Team)
Yahoo! Sports All-America Team (First Team)
SEC Coaches All-SEC (First Team)

BARRETT JONES
Outland Trophy Winner
Wuerffel Trophy Winner
Jacobs Blocking Trophy Winner
Capital One Academic First-Team All-American
AFCA FBS Coaches' All-America Team (First Team)
AP All-America Team (First Team)
FWAA All-America Team (First Team)
Sporting News All-America Team (First Team)
Walter Camp All-America Team (First Team)
ESPN.com's All-America Team (First Team)
CBSSports.com All-America Team (First Team)
SI.com All-America Team (First Team)
First-Team All-SEC (Coaches and AP)

DRE KIRKPATRICK
AP All-America Team (Second Team)
Pro Football Weekly All-America Team (First Team)
CBSSports.com All-America Team (First Team)
FWAA All-America Team (First Team)

CYRUS KOUANDJIO
Freshman All-SEC (Coaches)

DEQUAN MENZIE
AFCA FBS Coaches' All-America Team (First Team)

TEAM
Disney Spirit Award
(accepted by Carson Tinker on behalf of the team)

MARK BARRON
Team Captain
Jim Thorpe Award Finalist
AFCA FBS Coaches' All-America Team (First Team)
AP All-America Team (First Team)
FWAA All-America Team (First Team)
Sporting News All-America Team (First Team)
Walter Camp All-America Team (First Team)
SI.com All-America Team (First Team)

TRENT RICHARDSON

Team Captain

Doak Walker Award Winner

Heisman Trophy Finalist (Third)

SEC Offensive Player of the Year (Coaches and AP)

AFCA FBS Coaches' All-America Team (First Team)

AP All-American (First Team)

FWAA All-America Team (First Team)

Sporting News All-America Team (First Team)

Walter Camp All-America Team (First Team)

SI.com All-America Team (First Team)

ESPN.com's All-America Team (First Team)

Pro Football Weekly All-America Team (First Team)

CBSSports.com All-America Team (First Team)

Yahoo! Sports All-America Team (First Team)

First-Team All-SEC (Coaches and AP)

VINNIE SUNSERI

Freshman All-SEC (Coaches)

COURTNEY UPSHAW

FWAA All-America Team (First Team)

Sporting News All-America Team (First Team)

SI.com All-America Team (First Team)

ESPN.com's All-America Team (First Team)

AP All-America Team (Second Team)

CBSSports.com All-America Team (First Team)

Pro Football Weekly All-America Team (First Team)

First-Team All-SEC (Coaches and AP)

WILLIAM VLACHOS

Walter Camp All-America Team (Second Team)

First-Team All-SEC (Coaches and AP)

In Orlando on Dec. 8, 2011, Alabama's Carson Tinker, right, accepts the Disney Spirit Award on behalf of the Crimson Tide football team from Faron Kelley, Disney Sports' director of marketing.

About The Author

As assistant athletic director for the University of Alabama Athletics Department, Tommy Ford oversees the A-Club Alumni Association and the Red Elephant clubs.

Ford, a native of Gadsden, Alabama, earned his B.S. in Finance from the University of Alabama in 1978 and his M.A. in Higher Education Administration from the University of Alabama in 1998.

As a student at Alabama from 1974-78, Ford served in the SGA Senate, Jasons and Kappa Alpha fraternity, and during his senior year was sports editor of the *Crimson White*. After graduating from the Capstone, Ford returned to Gadsden before coming back to the university in 1982.

From 1982-87, Ford worked for the National Alumni Association in alumni chapter development and fundraising. In 1987, he was hired as assistant ticket manager in the Athletic Department, and then was promoted to ticket manager, for which he served from 1987-93. For 13 years from 1993-2006, Ford was director of TIDE PRIDE, the Athletic Department's football and basketball ticket priority program.

Ford is the author or co-author of four books: *Alabama's Family Tides*, *The University of Alabama All-Access Football Vault*, the *Alabama-Auburn Rivalry Football Vault* and *Bear Bryant on Leadership*.

Ford is married to the former Robin Rich of Gadsden, and the couple has one son, 15-year-old John Michael.

Author Acknowledgments

I want to thank several people for their contributions to *Tornado to National Title #14*.

First and foremost, to my friend Mark Mayfield, who assisted me with much of the tornado research, as well as editing my manuscript.

To Kent Gidley — who may have witnessed more University of Alabama athletic events than anyone in history — for his tireless work behind the camera lens and in front of the computer screen. With the exception of one photo, every image in this book was captured by Kent or one of his able assistants: Amelia J. Brackin, Jeri A. Gulsby and Lyndsey Pugh. The tornado funnel cloud photo was taken by Michelle Lepianka Carter of *The Tuscaloosa News*.

To assistant coaches Kirby Smart and Jim McElwain for their exclusive interviews for the BCS National Championship Game story. Their insight into Alabama's defensive and offensive game plans was fascinating and eye opening.

To ESPN's Brad Edwards, an Alabama alum, who so eloquently put into layman's terms the Crimson Tide's margin of "victory" over Oklahoma State in the decisive BCS standings.

To Jeff Purinton and Josh Maxson in UA Media Relations for their research assistance. To Thad Turnipseed for his help with Nick's Kids information.

To Finus Gaston, Alabama's senior associate athletic director and chief financial officer, for his making possible this project with Whitman Publishing.

And finally, to Terry Saban for pouring her heart out in the extraordinary foreword in the front of this book. She says the English teacher "came out in her," and for that we are all grateful. Roll Tide!

About The Photographer

As director of photography for the University of Alabama Athletics Department, Kent Gidley oversees all photography and photo archives.

Gidley, a native of Hokes Bluff, Alabama, earned his B.A. in Sports Photojournalism/Art from the University of Alabama in 1991.

Gidley began his post-secondary education at Gadsden State Community College on a vocal music scholarship. He then transferred to the University of Alabama in 1986. As a student at Alabama, Gidley served as an intern in the Sports Information Department as a student photographer, and was hired full time before graduating. After graduating from the Capstone, Gidley remained on staff as the first full-time Athletics Department photographer, a position he has held since

1988. Gidley also serves as an adjunct instructor of photography at the University of Alabama College of Communication and Information Sciences. He was awarded the Tom Tumlin Outstanding Achievement Award and the Sarah L. Healy Award for outstanding dedication and service in the field of publications.

Gidley's photographs have appeared in numerous national magazines and books, including *Sports Illustrated*, *The Sporting News*, *USA Today* and *The University of Alabama All-Access Football Vault*.

Gidley is married to the former KaKa Jones of Cullman, Alabama (former captain and graduate assistant coach of the University of Alabama cheerleading squad). The couple has three daughters, Loree M'Kay (10), K'Ten Marie (9) and Karis J'Myn (7), who are involved in gymnastics, running, softball and piano. The Gidleys are active members of Big Sandy Baptist Church, where Kent serves as a deacon.

Autographs

Autographs

Autographs

Autographs

Autographs

Autographs

Autographs

Autographs